150 S

TO GREATNESS

Insights from the world's top performers, distilled from the TALK4 Podcast, into actionable secrets to transform your life

**By
Louis Skupien**

Copyright © 2024 by Louis Skupien

All rights reserved.

No part of this publication may be reproduced, distributed, or transmitted in any form or by any means, including photocopying, recording, or other electronic or mechanical methods, without the prior written permission of the publisher, except in the case of brief quotations embodied in critical reviews and certain other non-commercial uses permitted by copyright law.

Disclaimer:

The views, lessons and key takeaways presented in this book are entirely my own interpretations of conversations held on the TALK4 Podcast. These reflections are generalised summaries based on my personal understanding of the insights I gained from the discussions. At no point do I directly quote the guests; rather, I distill the key messages and best lessons learned from our talks.

The guests featured in this book willingly participated in the TALK4 podcast and agreed to the distribution of their episodes on monetised platforms, including but not limited to YouTube, Spotify and Apple Podcasts. Many of the guests have signed agreements granting permission for their episodes to be published online. None of the guests requested that the conversations remain exclusive or undistributed. Promotion for their individual respective projects, businesses and websites can be found at the end of the book between pages **205-214**. Many of the guests in this book have reviewed their chapter and gave blessing to use their links and wording.

The structure and interpretation of this book are entirely my own and do not reflect the exact words or official positions of the podcast guests. The author assumes full responsibility for the content of this book and makes no claims as to the views or statements of the guests, beyond what was publicly discussed during their appearance on the podcast.

For permissions requests, please contact the publisher at:

louis@louisskupien.com

ISBN: 9798300639266

FOREWORD

By Jon Fay, Former Executive Officer of the U.S. Navy Blue Angels

Stories have a unique power—they lift us, guide us and reveal not just who we are but the limitless heights we can achieve. As a former Blue Angel, I've seen firsthand how narratives of courage, resilience and integrity serve as moving guidelines, charting courses toward greatness. Great stories are not just compelling; they are inspiring. They are beacons of effective leadership and character building. That's why I'm thrilled about what Louis Skupien, the Talk4 Podcast and *150 Secrets to Greatness* bring to the table.

The Talk4 podcast is more than a series of interviews. By sharing the insights and experiences of remarkable individuals, both celebrated and unsung, Louis has created a platform where themes like leadership, character and resilience are showcased. With its unique four-question format, Talk4 delivers concise, high-impact lessons that leave listeners ready to soar toward their own potential.

With *150 Secrets to Greatness*, Louis distills the wisdom of 30 podcast episodes (and counting) into actionable insights that serve as waypoints for personal and professional growth. The guests featured in *150 Secrets to Greatness* come from a variety of fields, but their trajectories share a common theme: they've used adversity, challenges and setbacks as fuel for high-performance and achievement. From elite commandos to world champion athletes, Top Gun fighter pilots to entrepreneurs, they've turned obstacles into opportunities and risen above, demonstrating that true greatness isn't achieved by luck, rather it is attained by

consistently leading with action, humility and a commitment to making a difference.

We live in a world hungry for authentic leadership and genuine role models—individuals who demonstrate values in the quiet moments when no one is watching. This book is packed with valuable lessons—a former Prisoner of War who survived 2,103 days in captivity with resilience and positivity, a Navy SEAL describing how they overcame impossible odds, or an entrepreneur candidly describing unlikely success achieved through failure. These aren't just stories— the book is packed with valuable lessons and guided reflection points, designed to help readers transform insights into actionable steps for becoming their best selves.

To Louis, thank you for building this platform and giving these voices the runway to take off. To every guest featured in Talk4 and this book, thank you for sharing your journeys and teaching us through your experiences. And to every reader, I hope these stories inspire you to climb higher, face challenges head-on and make your own positive impact in the world.

Every story here is a lesson—a chance to chart your course, rise above and reach new horizons.

Glad To Be Here,

Jon Fay

TABLE OF CONTENTS

Acknowledgements 1

Prologue 13

Chapter 1: Captain Charlie Plumb *A Vietnam Prisoner Of War's Lessons In Mental Strength* 17

Chapter 2: Ramon "CZ" Colon Lopez *Lessons From The SEAC On How To Lead* 25

Chapter 3: Mark Ormrod *Positivity In The Face Of Adversity* 31

Chapter 4: Neil Brown Jr *Embracing Versatility & Resilience As An Actor* 39

Chapter 5: Eddie Hamilton *Editing Movies At The Top Of Hollywood* 45

Chapter 6: Michelle "Mace" Curran *Thunderbird To Inspirational Speaking* 51

Chapter 7: Kegan "Smurf" Gill *Defying IMPOSSIBLE Odds And Coming Out On Top* 57

Chapter 8: Rich Graham *From Navy SEAL to Building the Full Spectrum Warrior* 63

Chapter 9: Mark Divine *The Warrior Mindset with Former Navy Seal Commander* 69

Chapter 10: Taylor "Fema" Hiester *Team Building Mastery* . 75

Chapter 11: Tucker "Cinco" Hamilton *An AI Insight From The U.S.A.F* 81

Chapter 12: Tyler Grey *The Pursuit Of Passion Will Make You A Winner* 87

Chapter 13: Eric Lee *What We Can Learn From What's Happened In The Music Industry* 93

Chapter 14: Anthony Smith *Mastering the Art of Video Storytelling* 99

Chapter 15: Kirk Lippold *When True Leadership Is Tested* 105

Chapter 16: Tim Parlatore *The Ethics Of Law & Basic Self Protection* 111

Chapter 17: Samuel "RaZZ" Larson *Flying The USA's Best Kept Military Secret* 117

Chapter 18: Greg Wooldridge *The Blueprint for Elite Teamwork and Leadership* 123

Chapter 19: Kris "Tanto" Paronto *Surviving Everything They Could Throw At Him* 129

Chapter 20: Trey Rawls *The Art of Leadership and Risk-Taking* 135

Chapter 21: Eddie Penney *The Tip Of The Spear In Anti-Terrorism* 141

Chapter 22: Lance Power Defending *The Free World From Cyber Threats* 147

Chapter 23: Matthew "Whiz" Buckley *Excelling In Top Gun & Business* 153

Chapter 24: Helen Isaac *Overcoming Adversity and Building a Fitness Legacy* 159

Chapter 25: Jon "Fizzle" Fay *Leading with Precision and Trust In The Blue Angels* 165

Chapter 26: Craig Harrison *Precision Defined By A Sniper World Record Holder* 171

Chapter 27: Miles Daisher *Jumping Off Everything So You Don't Have To!* 177

Chapter 28: Michael Sarraille *Leadership From A Navy SEAL* 183

Chapter 29: Joshua "Cabo" Gunderson *Lessons in Leadership, Inspiration and the Raptor's Legacy* 189

Chapter 30: Justin "Astro" Elliott *Turning The Thunderbirds Around* 195

Conclusion 201

Glossary of Key Terms, Organisations and Concepts 219

ACKNOWLEDGEMENTS

This book is a culmination of countless conversations, reflections and moments of inspiration. It wouldn't have been possible without the incredible support of many people along the way.

First and foremost, I want to extend my deepest gratitude to the guests of *Talk4* who generously shared their time, wisdom and stories. Each of you brought unique insights that not only shaped this book but have also impacted countless lives. Your willingness to engage in these meaningful conversations and to share your journeys openly is something I will forever appreciate. From military heroes and Hollywood stars to fitness experts and leaders in various industries, you have all contributed to making this project an unforgettable experience. Thank you for your trust and collaboration.

To the *Talk4* viewers and listeners, thank you for your unwavering support. This community is what drives me to keep pushing forward and bringing the best possible content to the world. Your engagement, feedback and passion for the show have been instrumental in its success. To everyone who has subscribed, left a comment, liked a video, or shared an episode with someone else — thank you for helping to grow this platform into something special.

To my family and friends, I am forever grateful for your constant encouragement, patience and love. You have supported me through every high and low and your belief in me has kept me motivated to continue chasing my dreams. Special thanks to my parents for instilling in me the values of hard work, resilience and determination.

Lastly, I want to thank everyone behind the scenes who has been instrumental in the production of this book. Your advice, expertise and dedication have helped bring this project to life.

This journey has been about more than just creating a book — it's been about learning, growing and connecting with so many extraordinary people. Thank you all for being part of it.

STAY CONNECTED

I'd love to hear from you and continue the conversation! You can find me across all major social media platforms:

- **Instagram**: @louisskupien
- **Twitter/X**: @louisskupien
- **YouTube**: @louisskupien
- **TikTok**: @louisskupien
- **LinkedIn**: @louisskupien

For all updates and new episodes, don't forget to check out *TALK4 Podcast* on:

- **Spotify**: TALK4 Podcast
- **Apple Podcast**: TALK4 Podcast
- **YouTube**: @louisskupien

Feel free to reach out with any thoughts, feedback, or just to say hello. I'm always open to new conversations and ideas!

LOUIS SKUPIEN

HOW TO USE AND READ MY BOOK:

Welcome to *150 Secrets To Greatness*! This book is designed to bring you insights and lessons from some of the world's most extraordinary individuals across various fields, from military leaders to Hollywood creatives and from elite athletes to renowned business experts. Here's how to make the most of your reading experience.

THE STRUCTURE OF EACH CHAPTER:

Every chapter follows a consistent and clear format, which is designed to help you absorb and apply the key lessons from each guest's episode. Here's how each chapter is laid out:

Introduction:

A brief overview of who the guest is, their background and why their insights are valuable. This will give you a sense of context for their experiences and expertise.

Episode Summary:

This section breaks down the core elements of the guest's story and conversation. It highlights pivotal moments in their life or career that define their approach to success, resilience and leadership. You'll gain a concise understanding of their journey and how they overcame challenges to become a top performer.

Five Key Lessons:

Each guest offers unique perspectives, but we distill the conversation into five key takeaways. These are actionable insights and ideas you can apply to your own life. These lessons are summarised based on the conversation but are my own interpretation of the core themes and ideas.

My Take:

Following each lesson, you'll find a brief reflection from me on how I personally interpreted and absorbed this wisdom. I share my thoughts to help you reflect on the guest's lessons in a more practical, everyday context. Think of it as a conversation with me on how these lessons can shape your own thinking.

Applying the Lessons to Life:

This section offers examples of how you can use the lessons from each guest in your daily life—whether in your career, personal development, or relationships. Here, I suggest steps and approaches to implementing what you've learned.

Reflection Questions:

To make the most of each chapter, it's important to reflect on how the lessons apply to your own journey. These questions are designed to prompt personal thought and introspection. Take the time to answer them, either mentally or by jotting them down in a journal. They're here to help you internalise the material.

Notes:

I encourage you to jot down thoughts, observations and action points you want to take forward. There's plenty of spare room on the pages to jot down thoughts!

LOUIS SKUPIEN

HOW TO APPROACH THIS BOOK:

One Chapter a Day:

To truly absorb and apply the lessons in this book, it's best to pace yourself. Try focusing on **one chapter per day**. By dedicating time to digest each guest's story, you give yourself room to reflect on the lessons and consider how they can apply to your own life. Remember, this book isn't about speed-reading but about *deep learning* and building lasting habits.

Reflect & Journal:

After reading a chapter, take some time to reflect on what stands out. The reflection questions are there to help you dig deeper into your personal thoughts and feelings about what you've learned.

Build a Habit:

Just like the top performers featured in this book, consistency is key. By making it a habit to read one chapter a day, you're committing to personal growth and self-improvement. This daily routine will compound over time and help you internalise the lessons, one small step at a time. Consistency is where the magic happens.

Apply the Lessons:

Knowledge is only as valuable as the action it inspires. After each chapter, try to incorporate one takeaway into your life. Start small, but be intentional. Whether it's adopting a new mindset, refining your leadership style, or tackling a specific challenge, you'll find that each chapter contains practical, actionable advice.

Reread and Revisit:

Don't be afraid to come back to chapters that resonate deeply with you. The journey of self-improvement isn't linear and sometimes it helps to revisit lessons as you grow. Each time you return to a chapter, you might find new insights that you hadn't noticed before.

Why One Chapter Per Day?

By pacing yourself at one chapter a day, you give yourself the opportunity to *absorb*, *reflect* and *apply*. These lessons are meant to inspire long-term transformation and growth. Taking it day by day allows the ideas to sink in and become a natural part of your daily habits and thought processes.

A Final Word:

Remember, this book is your guide, but the real transformation comes from *within*. The guests 'stories are here to inspire you, but how you apply them in your life is where the real impact will be. By committing to reading one chapter a day, reflecting on the lessons and implementing the key takeaways, you're setting yourself up for meaningful growth.

Let's go!

PROLOGUE

When I first sat down to record my podcast, *TALK4*, I had no idea just how far it would take me. What started as a simple idea—having honest conversations with fascinating individuals—quickly became something much larger. It wasn't just about asking questions; it was about digging deeper into the lives and minds of people who have reached the pinnacle of their fields. Whether it's a fighter pilot pulling Gs in an aerial combat manoeuvre, a special forces commander leading a mission against insurmountable odds, or an actor thriving in the spotlight, every guest has taught me something extraordinary. And now, those lessons are coming together in this book.

My name is Louis Skupien and I've always been someone with an intense desire to push boundaries. I grew up chasing excellence, whether it was in professional tennis, flying jets, or building businesses. My journey has been a whirlwind of challenges, extreme experiences and unforgettable moments. As a former professional tennis player, entrepreneur, content creator and personal trainer, I've always thrived on performance—finding ways to optimise myself and those around me. But through it all, *TALK4* became something unique, not just for me but for the thousands of people tuning in to hear the stories of remarkable individuals who have achieved greatness.

The podcast was born from my relentless curiosity. I wanted to know what drives people to be the best. What makes a Top Gun fighter pilot wake up every day and do the unthinkable? How does an elite military commander handle the mental weight of decisions that affect lives? And how can all of us, in our everyday lives, apply the same strategies to rise above our own challenges? Those questions fuelled *TALK4* and the answers I received have been nothing short of life-changing.

Over time, as the podcast grew, I realised there was more to be said, more to be shared than just the episodes alone. This book is an extension of that journey. It's for everyone who's ever tuned in to listen, but also for anyone looking to unlock their potential, to learn from the best and to apply those lessons in their own lives.

Inside this book, each chapter takes you on a deep dive into one of my podcast episodes. You'll get an inside look at the conversation, my personal reflections and, most importantly, the core takeaways that can help you make real, tangible changes in your life. Each guest has brought something different to the table, whether it's resilience in the face of adversity, the discipline of mastering a craft, or the mindset it takes to keep going when others would quit.

These aren't just stories of success. They are blueprints for overcoming obstacles, pushing beyond limitations and living life with purpose. You'll find actionable steps, distilled wisdom and real-world applications in every chapter—so you can put these lessons to work in your own journey, no matter where you are starting from.

Throughout my life, I've been fortunate to meet incredible people, but what stands out the most is their ability to inspire. This book captures that inspiration and delivers it to you. Whether you're looking to excel in your career, sharpen your mindset, or simply be a better version of yourself, you'll find what you need here.

So why this book and why now? Because I believe that greatness is not just for the elite—it's for anyone willing to put in the work, embrace the process and learn from those who have walked the path before. These lessons have helped shape my life and my work and now I want them to shape yours.

As you read on, I hope you'll feel the same spark I've felt sitting across from these guests—one that ignites the passion to chase something more. Because that's what this book is about: more than success, more than fame. It's about learning how to lead a life of purpose and fulfilment, no matter where you're starting from. Welcome to the journey and welcome to *Talk4* in print.

This is just the beginning.

Sic Parvis Magna

LOUIS SKUPIEN

CHAPTER 1: CAPTAIN CHARLIE PLUMB
A VIETNAM PRISONER OF WAR'S LESSONS IN MENTAL STRENGTH

INTRODUCTION

Captain Charlie Plumb is a man whose story goes beyond resilience; it's a testament to the power of choice in the face of extreme adversity. As a Navy fighter pilot who flew 74 combat missions in Vietnam, his life changed dramatically on his 75th mission when he was shot down and captured. What followed was 2,103 days of imprisonment in a Vietnamese prison camp. What struck me most during our conversation wasn't just the incredible physical ordeal he survived, but the mental transformation he underwent during those years. His ability to regain control of his mindset, even in the darkest of situations, is something we can all learn from. This chapter isn't just about Charlie's survival; it's about the lessons we can take from his story and apply to our own lives, no matter what challenges we face.

EPISODE SUMMARY

Charlie's early life didn't exactly scream "future fighter pilot." Growing up in the middle of Kansas, he had no experience with aviation and no one in his family had served in the military. But after gaining an appointment to the U.S. Naval Academy, his path took a sharp turn toward the skies. His career eventually led him to become one of the founding members of the Top Gun programme, where he trained in supersonic jets and prepared for the dangerous missions ahead in Vietnam.

On his 75th mission, just days before he was due to return home, Charlie's jet was hit by a surface-to-air missile. He ejected, landing in enemy territory, where he was quickly captured. For the next six years, Charlie was subjected to unimaginable physical pain and psychological torment. But what stands out most from his story is that his biggest battle wasn't against his captors—it was in his mind.

At his lowest point, Charlie was consumed by guilt, shame and the belief that he had failed. But it was through clandestine communication with other prisoners that he realised he still had one crucial thing left—his ability to choose his mindset. It was this revelation that allowed him to turn the situation around and find meaning in what seemed like a hopeless situation.

When he was finally released in 1973, Charlie returned home a changed man. He used the lessons he learned during his imprisonment to shape his life, eventually becoming a speaker and sharing his powerful message of resilience and personal choice with audiences around the world.

FIVE KEY LESSONS

1. You Always Have a Choice

One of the most powerful lessons I took away from my conversation with Charlie is that no matter how dire the circumstances, you always have a choice. It's easy to think that when everything is taken away from you—your freedom, your comfort, your control—you're left powerless. But Charlie's story taught me that even in the worst situations, you still have control over one thing: your mindset. He could have given in to despair, but instead, he chose to fight, not with fists, but with his mind.

My Take:

In life, we all face situations where we feel trapped, whether it's in a job, a relationship, or a personal struggle. The key is to remember that no matter how stuck we feel, there's always a choice to be made. It might not be about changing the situation itself, but how we respond to it. Ask yourself, "What can I control right now? How can I change my perspective?" By taking ownership of your mindset, you take the first step towards freedom.

2. Resilience is Built Through Adversity

Charlie's story is the ultimate testament to resilience. What really struck me was how he didn't just endure his six years of captivity—he grew from it. He transformed one of the worst experiences a human could face into something that made him stronger. This wasn't about avoiding pain or suffering—it was about accepting it, learning from it and letting it shape him for the better.

My Take:

Adversity isn't something we can avoid in life, but how we deal with it defines who we become. The next time you face a setback or a challenge, instead of asking, "Why me?", try asking, "What can I learn from this?" When you shift your mindset to see adversity as an opportunity for growth, you'll find that every tough situation has something to offer.

3. Leadership and Teamwork Matter in Tough Times

What amazed me about Charlie's time in the prison camp was how crucial his connection with other prisoners was. Even when they couldn't see each other, they found ways to communicate through secret codes. They encouraged each other, shared their strength and lifted each other up when it would have been easy to fall into despair. That sense of leadership and teamwork played a huge role in their survival.

My Take:

This lesson hit home for me. No matter how tough things get, it's the people around you who can help you get through. Whether it's family, friends, or colleagues, building and nurturing those connections is crucial. Don't try to go it alone. Surround yourself with people who will push you forward and be there for you when times get tough.

4. Mental Toughness Can Break Physical Limits

Another key takeaway from Charlie's story was the realisation that the greatest prison he faced wasn't the physical one—it was the mental one. He told me that once he mastered his mindset, his body's suffering became more bearable. Mental toughness isn't just about enduring pain—it's about choosing how to react to it.

My Take:

Life is full of moments that push us to our physical or emotional limits. But Charlie's experience shows that it's the mind that determines how far we can go. We often limit ourselves mentally before we're actually limited physically. Focus on developing mental resilience, whether through mindfulness, meditation, or simply challenging yourself to push beyond what you think are your limits. You'll be amazed at what you can achieve.

5. Forgiveness is a Tool for Survival

One of the things that really stuck with me was how Charlie spoke about forgiveness—not just as a moral act, but as a survival tool. Early on, he was consumed with anger and bitterness toward his captors. But over time, he realised that holding onto that anger wasn't hurting them—it was hurting him. Letting go of that bitterness allowed him to focus on surviving and eventually thriving.

My Take:

It's easy to hold onto grudges and let anger fester, but doing so only holds you back. Forgiveness isn't about excusing the wrongs done to you; it's about freeing yourself from the emotional weight they carry. If there's someone or something you're holding a grudge against, consider what it's really costing you. Start by asking yourself, "How is this anger serving me?" Often, the act of forgiveness is the first step toward real freedom.

APPLYING THE LESSONS TO LIFE

The lessons I've taken from Charlie's story are powerful, but they're only useful if we put them into practice. Here's how you can start applying these lessons in your own life:

- **Identify your choices:** Think of a situation in your life where you feel stuck or powerless. Now, take a moment to reflect. What choices do you still have? Maybe it's not about changing the situation, but changing how you think about it. Write down three possible choices you could make in this scenario, even if they seem small.

- **Strengthen your resilience:** Look back on a challenging moment in your life—something that felt impossible to get through at the time. What did you learn from that experience? How did it change you for the better? Now, think about a current challenge and ask yourself, "What lesson is there for me in this?"

- **Build your support network:** Who are the people in your life that you can rely on when things get tough? List three people you can turn to for support. If you don't have anyone, how can you start building those connections? Don't wait until you're in a crisis—strengthen those relationships now.

- **Develop mental toughness:** Start by building small mental challenges into your daily routine. Whether it's through meditation, pushing yourself a little harder in a workout, or simply practising patience when things don't go your way, focus on mastering your mind. Keep track of how you react to stress and see how you can improve.

- **Practice forgiveness:** Is there someone or something you're holding a grudge against? Ask yourself whether holding onto that anger is serving you or holding you back. Write down one small step you can take toward letting go—whether it's having a conversation, writing a letter you'll never send, or simply deciding to stop dwelling on it.

APPLY THE LESSONS: REFLECTION QUESTIONS

Take some time to reflect on how Charlie's lessons apply to your life:

1. What choices do I have in my current challenge?
2. How has adversity shaped me in the past and how can I use that to my advantage now?
3. Who is part of my support network and how can I nurture those relationships?
4. What steps can I take to develop mental toughness?
5. Who or what do I need to forgive and how can I begin that process?

Website, links, projects & contact available on pages 205-214

LOUIS SKUPIEN

CHAPTER 2: RAMON "CZ" COLON LOPEZ
LESSONS FROM THE SEAC ON HOW TO LEAD

INTRODUCTION

Ramón "CZ" Colón-López, a 33-year military veteran, served as the Senior Enlisted Advisor to the Chairman of the Joint Chiefs of Staff (SEAC). With a career rooted in Special Operations, Colón-López worked directly with top U.S. defence leaders, including the Secretary of Defence and the President of the United States. His remarkable journey from Puerto Rico to the highest enlisted position in the U.S. military is filled with lessons on discipline, leadership and growth. In this chapter, we explore Colón-López's path to becoming one of the most respected leaders in the military and how his experiences can inspire us to build resilience, foster accountability and lead with integrity.

EPISODE SUMMARY

Ramón "CZ" Colón-López's military career is marked by both early challenges and significant achievements. Born in Puerto Rico, he moved to the United States as a teenager and struggled to adapt to his new environment, particularly with language barriers. After some years in college, he sought more structure in his life and joined the military. Colón-López's initial enlistment was not driven by a sense of purpose but rather a need for discipline. However, it wasn't long before he found his calling within the Special Operations community.

Throughout his career, Colón-López encountered challenges, including disciplinary setbacks. However, instead of letting these obstacles define him, he used them as opportunities for growth. Over time, he ascended to the role of Senior Enlisted Advisor to the Chairman of the Joint Chiefs of Staff, where he advised senior leaders on matters ranging from combat readiness to global defence strategies. Colón-López's leadership style is grounded in humility, accountability and an unwavering commitment to excellence. His experiences offer invaluable insights for leaders in any field, from the military to business and beyond.

FIVE KEY LESSONS

1. The Importance of Structure and Discipline

Colón-López's initial reason for joining the military was to find structure in his life. After facing personal dissatisfaction, he realised that he needed discipline to fulfil his potential. This decision marked the beginning of his transformation from an unfulfilled college student to a highly respected leader.

My Take:

Structure and discipline are key to success in any endeavour. By committing to personal discipline, you can create the foundation for growth and achievement in both your personal and professional life.

2. Embrace Failure and Learn from It

Early in his military career, Colón-López faced disciplinary action that almost ended his service. Instead of being discouraged, he took responsibility for his actions, learned from his mistakes and used the experience to fuel his growth. His ability to overcome adversity was a crucial step in his leadership journey.

My Take:

Failure is a powerful teacher. When we own our mistakes and use them as learning opportunities, we set ourselves up for long-term success. Growth comes from facing challenges head-on, not avoiding them.

3. Lead by Example

As a leader, Colón-López believes in setting the example for others to follow. Whether it was maintaining his physical fitness or adhering to the highest standards of conduct, he understood that actions speak louder than words. His leadership philosophy is based on showing, not just telling.

My Take:

The most effective leaders are those who lead by example. People are more likely to follow you if they see you embody the values and behaviours you expect from them.

4. Invest in People and Relationships

Throughout his career, Colón-López sought out mentors and role models who could help him grow. He understood the importance of building relationships and learning from those who had achieved success. This helped him develop both as a leader and a person.

My Take:

Success is rarely achieved in isolation. Surround yourself with people who inspire and challenge you and invest in building strong relationships. Mentorship is a powerful tool for personal and professional growth.

5. Cultural Investment and Accountability

Colón-López emphasises the importance of being culturally invested in your organisation. Leaders must hold themselves and their teams accountable to high standards and never turn a blind eye to problems. His success as a leader came from his ability to foster a culture of accountability and shared responsibility.

My Take:

Accountability is the cornerstone of a strong team. When everyone is committed to the same high standards, the team can operate more effectively. Leaders must set the tone and ensure that everyone is working toward the same goals.

APPLYING THE LESSONS TO LIFE

Ramón "CZ" Colón-López's journey offers valuable lessons that anyone can apply to their life and career. Here are some practical ways to use his principles:

- **Commit to discipline:** Whether it's in your personal or professional life, establishing a routine and maintaining discipline can set the foundation for success.

- **Turn failure into growth:** When faced with challenges, embrace them as opportunities to learn and grow, rather than as setbacks.

- **Lead by example:** In every aspect of life, whether at home, work, or in your community, be the example that others can look up to.

- **Seek out mentors:** Find people who inspire you and can guide you on your journey. Invest in relationships that will help you grow.

- **Foster a culture of accountability:** Whether you're leading a team or working as part of one, hold yourself and others to the highest standards of responsibility and performance.

APPLY THE LESSONS: REFLECTION QUESTIONS

1. How can you introduce more structure and discipline into your daily routine to improve your effectiveness?

2. What past failures can you reframe as learning opportunities to help you move forward?

3. Are you leading by example in your personal and professional life? What areas could benefit from you stepping up as a role model?

4. Who are the mentors or role models you can turn to for guidance? How can you actively seek out their advice and learn from their experiences?

5. How can you create a culture of accountability in your team or organisation?

Website, links, projects & contact available on pages 205-214

CHAPTER 3: MARK ORMROD
POSITIVITY IN THE FACE OF ADVERSITY

INTRODUCTION

Mark Ormrod's story is one of extraordinary resilience, mental toughness and an unrelenting drive to push the boundaries of what's possible. A Royal Marines Commando, Mark's life changed forever in 2007 when he stepped on an improvised explosive device (IED) during a routine patrol in Afghanistan. He lost both legs and his right arm in the blast. Despite the unimaginable trauma, Mark defied the odds, becoming the UK's first triple amputee to survive the Afghanistan conflict. Today, he is an Invictus Games champion, motivational speaker and a symbol of overcoming the most extreme adversity. This chapter dives into Mark's journey from that fateful day, the mindset that propelled him forward and the lessons we can take from his experience to apply to our own lives.

EPISODE SUMMARY

Mark Ormrod's journey began long before his military career. Growing up in Plymouth, Mark was inspired by action films and the stories of older friends who had joined the military. After receiving guidance from his uncle, who served in the Royal Marines, Mark decided to enlist at just 16 years old. By 2001, at the age of 17, Mark had joined the Royal Marines, facing the rigorous training required to earn the coveted Green Beret.

His career took him across various operations, including a deployment to Iraq in 2003. While Iraq didn't provide the combat experience Mark had anticipated, his commitment to the Marines remained unwavering. After a brief stint away from the military, Mark rejoined the Royal Marines in 2007, just in time for a deployment to Afghanistan.

On Christmas Eve 2007, while on patrol in Helmand Province, Mark knelt on an IED, losing both legs and his right arm in the explosion. Remarkably, Mark remained conscious throughout the ordeal and vividly recalls the moments immediately following the blast. Despite being declared dead twice during his evacuation, the medical team managed to revive him. Mark's recovery was gruelling, both physically and mentally, but he refused to accept the limitations placed on him by his injuries. Over time, he learned to walk again with prosthetics, becoming the UK's first triple amputee to do so without using a wheelchair.

Since then, Mark has gone on to achieve extraordinary feats, including winning 11 medals in the Invictus Games, becoming a purple belt in Brazilian Jiu-Jitsu and raising millions for military charities. His story is a testament to the power of resilience, mindset and the unwavering belief that we are capable of far more than we think.

FIVE KEY LESSONS

1. Resilience is Built Through Adversity

Mark's journey to recovery was anything but smooth. The physical pain and emotional toll were overwhelming, yet he persevered, step by step. What stood out most during our conversation was Mark's understanding that resilience isn't something you're born with—it's something you develop by facing and overcoming challenges.

My Take:

Adversity is a part of life, but how we respond to it shapes who we become. Mark's story reminds me that resilience is built over time, through consistent effort and the decision to keep moving forward, even when it feels impossible. When life throws challenges your way, remember that each obstacle is an opportunity to strengthen your resilience.

2. The Power of Purpose

After his injury, Mark had to redefine his sense of purpose. For someone who had lived as an elite military operator, the loss of physical ability could have easily led to despair. But instead, Mark channeled his energy into becoming the best version of himself, setting new goals and refusing to be defined by his injuries.

My Take:

Finding your purpose is key to overcoming adversity. Whether it's in your career, relationships, or personal development, having a strong "why" helps you navigate difficult times. When life feels uncertain, ask yourself: what is my purpose? What goal can I strive towards, no matter the circumstances? With a clear purpose, even the hardest challenges can become stepping stones toward growth.

3. Break It Down, Day by Day

Mark talked about the overwhelming nature of Royal Marines training and his rehabilitation. Rather than focus on the long-term, he learned to break things down into manageable chunks—sometimes just getting through the next hour was the goal. This mindset was crucial during his recovery.

My Take:

When faced with a seemingly insurmountable challenge, don't focus on the entire journey. Instead, break it down into smaller, achievable tasks. Whether it's recovering from an injury, starting a new project, or tackling a major life change, taking things step by step makes the process more manageable and less overwhelming.

4. Mental Toughness is Essential

Mark's story is a powerful reminder of the importance of mental toughness. It wasn't just his body that needed to heal—it was his mind. He had to believe that recovery was possible, even when it felt impossible. His military training taught him to stay disciplined and push through the pain, but it was his mental strength that truly carried him through.

My Take:

Mental toughness isn't about pretending everything is okay—it's about acknowledging the difficulty of the situation and choosing to keep going anyway. Whether you're facing physical pain, emotional challenges, or difficult life circumstances, strengthening your mind will allow you to push through your perceived limits.

5. The Value of Community and Support

Mark emphasised the role that his friends, family and military community played in his recovery. From the Royal Marines to the charities that supported him, Mark was surrounded by people who pushed him forward, offering guidance and mentorship along the way.

My Take:

No one achieves greatness alone. Building a strong support network is crucial for getting through tough times. Whether it's friends, family, or colleagues, lean on the people who believe in you and encourage you to keep going. Likewise, be that support for others—helping others through their challenges can give you strength in your own journey.

APPLYING THE LESSONS TO LIFE

The lessons from Mark's story are powerful, but they're only useful if we put them into practice. Here's how you can apply these lessons in your life:

- **Build resilience:** Reflect on a challenging situation you've faced. How did you handle it? What did you learn? Use that experience to fuel your response to future challenges.

- **Clarify your purpose:** Take some time to define your purpose. What drives you? What are your goals? Write down one thing you're striving for and remind yourself of it when times get tough.

- **Break it down:** Identify a large goal or challenge you're currently facing. Now break it into smaller, manageable tasks. Focus on completing one task at a time rather than being overwhelmed by the whole process.

- **Strengthen your mind:** Find ways to cultivate mental toughness. This could be through meditation, physical training, or simply challenging yourself to push through discomfort. Track your progress and celebrate small victories.

- **Lean on your community:** Who are the people in your life who support you? Make a list of three people you can turn to for encouragement. If you don't have a support system, think about how you can build one.

APPLY THE LESSONS: REFLECTION QUESTIONS

Take some time to reflect on how Mark's lessons apply to your life:

1. How have I demonstrated resilience in the past and how can I apply that to my current challenges?

2. What is my purpose and how can it guide me through adversity?

3. What's one large goal I can break into smaller steps to make it more manageable?

4. How can I develop greater mental toughness in my daily life?

5. Who can I turn to for support and how can I strengthen those relationships?

Website, links, projects & contact available on pages 205-214

LOUIS SKUPIEN

CHAPTER 4: NEIL BROWN JR
EMBRACING VERSATILITY & RESILIENCE AS AN ACTOR

INTRODUCTION

Neil Brown Jr. is an actor who has made a name for himself in the world of film and television, particularly through his role as Ray Perry on the hit show *SEAL Team*. But Neil's journey into acting was anything but conventional. From his early days as a martial artist and boxer to becoming a seasoned actor, Neil's path is a testament to the importance of perseverance, adaptability and staying true to one's passion. In this chapter, we'll explore Neil's unique journey into acting, his experiences portraying complex characters and the life lessons that have shaped both his career and his approach to life.

EPISODE SUMMARY

Neil Brown Jr.'s journey into acting began with a surprising twist. He was a young martial artist and boxer, training for competitions and spending most of his time in the gym. After getting into trouble at school, Neil found himself training at the dojo when a producer happened to walk in. A chance encounter led Neil to audition for a TV show, despite having no prior acting experience. His natural talent and ability to memorise lines quickly won him the role and from that moment on, Neil was hooked on acting.

Though he initially envisioned a career in the military, Neil realised that acting allowed him to live out many of the roles he admired in action movies—without the real-life consequences. His early exposure to martial arts and discipline carried over into his acting career, helping him land roles in action-packed films and TV shows, including *Battle: Los Angeles* and *SEAL Team*.

When the opportunity to audition for *SEAL Team* came along, Neil was ready. Having grown up in a military family and with years of experience in physically demanding roles, he felt an immediate connection to the character of Ray Perry. Neil's performance quickly resonated with audiences and his portrayal of Ray has become one of the standout elements of the series.

Over the years, Neil has developed a deep understanding of Ray Perry, both as a character and as a reflection of the real-life challenges faced by special operators. From the physical training required to portray a Navy SEAL to the emotional depth needed for some of the show's most intense scenes, Neil's dedication to his craft shines through in every episode.

FIVE KEY LESSONS

1. Seize Opportunities, Even When They're Unexpected

Neil's entry into acting was anything but planned. He didn't set out to become an actor, but when the opportunity presented itself, he took a leap of faith. That chance encounter in the dojo changed the course of his life.

My Take:

Sometimes life throws opportunities our way when we least expect them. The key is to be open to new possibilities and have the courage to take the leap when they arise. Whether it's a career shift, a new relationship, or an unexpected project, saying "yes" to the unknown can lead to incredible growth.

2. Preparation Meets Opportunity

Neil's background in martial arts and boxing gave him the physical foundation he needed for many of his roles. Years of discipline, training and honing his skills meant that when the right opportunity came along, he was ready to step up.

My Take:

Success often comes when preparation meets opportunity. It's not just about being lucky—it's about being prepared for when luck strikes. Whatever your craft, whether it's in your career or personal life, invest in your skills and stay ready for when the moment arrives.

3. Vulnerability is a Strength

One of the most striking elements of Neil's portrayal of Ray Perry is his ability to show vulnerability, even as a tough Navy SEAL. Whether it's during emotionally charged scenes or moments of reflection, Neil emphasises that being vulnerable makes a character—and a person—more relatable and real.

My Take:

Being vulnerable isn't a sign of weakness—it's a sign of strength. It takes courage to open up and let others see your true self, especially in a world that often celebrates toughness over tenderness. Embracing vulnerability can lead to deeper connections and more authentic experiences, both on screen and in life.

4. Patience and Perseverance are Key

Neil's journey hasn't been without its challenges. After going through multiple pilot seasons and not landing roles, Neil had to learn the importance of patience and perseverance. His advice to actors and anyone pursuing their dreams is to understand that success doesn't happen overnight—it's a marathon, not a sprint.

My Take:

Life's biggest achievements don't happen instantly. Whether you're pursuing a career, working towards a personal goal, or overcoming adversity, patience and perseverance are crucial. Trust the process, keep putting in the work and don't be discouraged by setbacks. Success will come in time.

5. Embrace Who You Are

Neil stressed the importance of bringing your unique experiences and personality to your roles. Rather than trying to fit into a mould, he encourages actors to use their individuality to create more authentic and compelling performances.

My Take:

We each have something unique to offer the world. Rather than trying to conform to what you think others expect of you, embrace who you are and let your individuality shine. Whether in your career, relationships, or personal projects, being true to yourself will always lead to more fulfilling outcomes.

APPLYING THE LESSONS TO LIFE

The lessons from Neil Brown Jr.'s story are powerful and applicable to anyone, whether or not they're in the entertainment industry. Here are some ways you can apply these lessons to your own life:

- **Seize the moment:** Think about an opportunity that you may have passed up or hesitated to take in the past. How might your life be different if you had said "yes"? Be open to new opportunities and trust yourself to make the most of them.

- **Stay prepared:** Identify a skill or area of your life that you want to improve. Commit to consistently working on it, so that when the right opportunity comes along, you'll be ready to take it on.

- **Be vulnerable:** In your next conversation or interaction, try letting your guard down a bit. Whether it's sharing a personal story or admitting a challenge you're facing, see how being vulnerable can deepen your connection with others.

- **Keep going:** If you're working towards a big goal, remind yourself that success takes time. Reflect on the progress you've made so far and stay committed to the journey, even if it's taking longer than you'd like.

- **Celebrate your uniqueness:** Take a moment to think about what makes you unique. What life experiences, skills, or perspectives do you bring to the table that others might not? Embrace those qualities and let them shine in everything you do.

APPLY THE LESSONS: REFLECTION QUESTIONS

Take some time to reflect on how Neil's lessons apply to your life:

1. What unexpected opportunities have come your way and how can you be more open to new ones in the future?

2. How are you preparing yourself for the next big opportunity in your career or personal life?

3. Where can you embrace vulnerability in your life and how might that strengthen your relationships?

4. What is a long-term goal you're working towards and how can you stay patient and persevering on the journey?

5. How can you celebrate your unique qualities and let them shine in your work or personal life?

Website, links, projects & contact available on pages 205-214

CHAPTER 5: EDDIE HAMILTON
EDITING MOVIES AT THE TOP OF HOLLYWOOD

INTRODUCTION

Eddie Hamilton is one of the most accomplished film editors in the industry, known for his meticulous work on high-octane blockbusters such as *Top Gun: Maverick*, *Mission: Impossible – Fallout* and *Kingsman*. With nearly 30 years of experience in the field, Eddie has become an expert in the art of storytelling through film editing. This chapter delves into his fascinating journey, his creative process and the invaluable insights he shared during our podcast episode.

EPISODE SUMMARY

Eddie's love for filmmaking began at an early age. Like many of us, he was deeply inspired by watching *Star Wars* as a child, but what set him apart was his ability to see beyond the magic of the screen to the people behind the scenes. At just eight years old, Eddie realised that making films was a career option and from that moment, he was captivated.

Growing up, Eddie dedicated himself to understanding the craft, reading as many books as he could and experimenting with editing by using two VHS machines. Despite not being accepted into film school, his passion for editing and storytelling never wavered. He began his career as a runner at a post-production house, slowly working his way up by teaching himself how to use editing software like Avid. His first major break came when he met director Matthew Vaughn and edited *Mean Machine*, a pivotal project that would lead to future collaborations on *Kick-Ass* and *Kingsman*.

Eddie's journey reached new heights when he was invited to work on *Mission: Impossible – Rogue Nation*. It was here that he met Tom Cruise, beginning a working relationship that would carry on through *Mission: Impossible – Fallout* and the critically acclaimed *Top Gun: Maverick*. Working with Tom Cruise and director Christopher McQuarrie allowed Eddie to explore the high-pressure world of big-budget filmmaking. Despite the challenges, he thrived, delivering finely crafted action sequences and emotionally engaging narratives.

FIVE KEY LESSONS

1. Passion Fuels Persistence

Eddie's career trajectory is a testament to the power of passion. From the moment he saw *Star Wars*, Eddie was determined to be a part of the film industry. Even after being rejected from film school, he didn't give up. Instead, he focused on gaining practical experience and learning on the job.

My Take:

Passion is what keeps you going when things don't go as planned. It's not just about talent—it's about having the drive to keep learning and improving. When you're truly passionate about something, every setback becomes a stepping stone towards achieving your goal.

2. Let the Footage Speak to You

Eddie's approach to editing is rooted in letting the raw footage dictate the flow and structure of a scene. Instead of imposing a specific style from the outset, he allows the material to guide him. This organic method ensures that the story remains authentic and that the best aspects of the footage shine through.

My Take:

Creativity isn't about forcing a vision; it's about being open to what emerges naturally. Whether you're editing a film, writing a book, or working on a project, sometimes the best outcomes come from letting the process unfold and responding to it in real-time.

3. Don't Be Afraid to Rework and Refine

According to Eddie, the first cut of a film is often rough and unfocused and that's okay. The true magic of editing comes from the ability to rework, refine and constantly improve a scene. He emphasises that the process of editing is long and detailed, but each pass brings the film closer to perfection.

My Take:

In any creative endeavour, the first draft is rarely the final product. The willingness to revisit and refine your work is crucial. By continually improving, you'll find the balance and clarity needed to achieve the best possible result.

4. Engage with the Audience

Eddie stressed the importance of screening a film for test audiences and listening to their feedback. He explained that when audiences feel confused, bored, or disengaged, it's vital to address these issues in the edit. This collaborative process helps ensure that the final product resonates with viewers.

My Take:

Feedback is a powerful tool. Whether it's in filmmaking or any other field, listening to your audience or customer base can provide invaluable insights. It's important to stay humble, accept criticism and make adjustments that enhance the overall experience for your audience.

5. Strive for Mastery

Eddie is deeply committed to excellence, constantly striving to be the best in his field. He works long hours and maintains a relentless focus on delivering the highest quality work possible. For him, it's not about shortcuts or quick fixes—it's about putting in the time and effort to master the craft.

My Take:

Mastery requires dedication. Whatever your profession, the only way to become great is by putting in the hours and continually pushing yourself to improve. Embrace the learning process, stay focused on your goals and never stop striving for excellence.

APPLYING THE LESSONS TO LIFE

Eddie Hamilton's experiences offer valuable lessons that can be applied far beyond the world of film editing. Here's how you can incorporate these insights into your own life:

- **Follow your passion:** If there's something you're deeply passionate about, commit to it fully. Even when obstacles arise, let your passion drive you forward.

- **Let go of perfectionism:** In any creative process, the first version won't be perfect. Embrace the idea that the real work comes in refining and improving what you've started.

- **Seek feedback:** Whether you're working on a project, business, or personal goal, don't be afraid to ask for feedback. It can provide fresh perspectives and help you make meaningful improvements.

- **Master your craft:** Set yourself on a path of continuous learning and improvement. Aim to be the best at what you do by putting in the time and effort required to truly master your skills.

APPLY THE LESSONS: REFLECTION QUESTIONS

To help apply these lessons, consider the following reflection questions:

1. What passion project have you been putting off and how can you start making progress on it today?

2. How do you typically approach feedback—are you open to it, or do you resist it? How can you use feedback more effectively?

3. What area of your life or work could benefit from more time spent refining and improving?

4. How can you structure your day to ensure that you're working towards mastering your craft, even if it's just a little each day?

Website, links, projects & contact available on pages 205-214

CHAPTER 6: MICHELLE "MACE" CURRAN
THUNDERBIRD TO INSPIRATIONAL SPEAKING

INTRODUCTION

Michelle Curran, known by her call sign "Mace," spent over a decade flying the F-16 fighter jet in the U.S. Air Force and she is widely recognised for her time as a solo pilot with the Thunderbirds, one of the most prestigious air demonstration teams in the world. In this chapter, we explore her unique journey, the challenges she overcame and the wisdom she shared about leadership, self-confidence and striving for excellence.

EPISODE SUMMARY

Michelle's path to becoming a fighter pilot wasn't the conventional one. Growing up in a small town in Wisconsin, she didn't come from a military or aviation background. However, her adventurous nature, combined with academic excellence, led her to apply for an Air Force ROTC scholarship in high school. Originally intending to serve her four years and then pursue a career in the FBI, her life took a sharp turn during a visit to a military base where she witnessed F-15s taking off at dusk. That experience ignited a passion for aviation and she soon set her sights on becoming a fighter pilot.

After excelling in pilot training, Michelle earned her top choice—the F-16 Fighting Falcon. She spent nearly a decade flying the aircraft in various combat and training roles before being selected for the prestigious Thunderbirds team. As the lead solo pilot, she became only the second woman in history to hold that role, showcasing her skills and leadership across the U.S. and internationally.

During her time with the Thunderbirds, Michelle had to navigate the physical and mental demands of being in the public eye, balancing high-intensity flying with extensive media and public engagement. Despite the challenges, she thrived, learning to manage her energy, develop a routine and overcome the self-doubt that had plagued her earlier in her career.

Today, Michelle has transitioned into a new role as a motivational speaker, children's author and coach, continuing to inspire people around the world. She speaks openly about her journey, offering practical advice on how to push past self-doubt, manage pressure and thrive in high-stakes environments.

FIVE KEY LESSONS

1. Trust Your Gut and Take the Leap

Michelle's career pivot from aspiring FBI agent to fighter pilot was driven by a gut feeling. After seeing the F-15s in action, she knew she had to follow her passion, even though it wasn't the path she initially planned. By trusting her instincts, she embraced a new opportunity that ultimately shaped her future.

My Take:

We all have moments where life presents us with a choice that feels daunting but exciting. It's in these moments that trusting your gut and taking that first step can lead to incredible outcomes. Don't be afraid to change direction if your heart tells you it's right.

2. Push Through Self-Doubt

Michelle admitted that she struggled with self-doubt early in her career, especially in the male-dominated fighter pilot community. However, she emphasised the importance of confronting those feelings and proving to yourself that you can overcome obstacles. Each challenge she faced—whether it was flying in combat zones or performing complex aerial manoeuvres—built her confidence and solidified her belief in her abilities.

My Take:

Self-doubt is natural, but it doesn't have to define your actions. The only way to build confidence is to tackle challenges head-on and show yourself that you're capable of more than you think. Start small, build momentum and you'll find that your confidence grows with every victory.

3. Manage Your Energy, Not Just Your Time

Being on the road 240 days a year with the Thunderbirds was exhausting, both physically and mentally. Michelle quickly realised that to perform at her best, she needed to manage her energy levels, not just her time. She developed routines, prioritised sleep, meal-prepped to maintain a healthy diet and learned to say no to non-essential activities in order to recharge.

My Take:

Productivity isn't just about working hard—it's about working smart. Managing your energy, especially in high-pressure environments, is key to avoiding burnout and sustaining long-term success. Find the routines that work for you and stick to them, even when it's tempting to let them slip.

4. Embrace the Role of Being a Role Model

As one of the few female fighter pilots, Michelle faced additional scrutiny and attention. Instead of shying away from the spotlight, she embraced her role as a role model. She shared her experiences openly on social media, offering a glimpse into both the highs and the struggles of her career, which made her relatable and inspiring to others.

My Take:

When you're in a position where others look up to you, it's important to recognise the impact you can have. By being authentic and vulnerable, you can inspire others who may be on a similar journey. Don't be afraid to step into the role of a mentor or leader—it can have a profound effect on those who follow in your footsteps.

5. Focus on Progress, Not Perfection

In the world of elite fighter pilots, striving for perfection is an endless pursuit. Michelle acknowledged that there's no such thing as a perfect flight—there will always be minor deviations and adjustments. What matters is consistently improving and learning from each experience to become better over time.

My Take:

Perfection is often an unattainable goal and focusing on it can lead to frustration. Instead, aim for progress. Celebrate the small victories, learn from mistakes and keep pushing forward. Consistent improvement will get you much further than chasing perfection.

APPLYING THE LESSONS TO LIFE

Michelle Curran's story provides several lessons that can be applied in all areas of life. Here are a few ways to incorporate these insights:

- **Take calculated risks:** Trust your instincts and don't be afraid to pursue a new direction if it aligns with your passions.

- **Build confidence through action:** Overcome self-doubt by tackling challenges head-on and proving to yourself that you can succeed.

- **Prioritise energy management:** Create routines that help you recharge and sustain your energy over the long term.

- **Lead by example:** Embrace your role as a role model, whether in your career or personal life, by being authentic and open with your experiences.

- **Celebrate progress:** Focus on improving bit by bit rather than striving for unattainable perfection.

APPLY THE LESSONS: REFLECTION QUESTIONS

Consider the following reflection questions to help apply these lessons in your own life:

1. What opportunities have you passed up because of self-doubt and how can you approach similar situations differently in the future?

2. How do you manage your energy levels during stressful periods and what routines could you implement to improve your performance?

3. In what ways can you serve as a role model or mentor to others, even if you're still on your own journey?

4. How can you shift your mindset from seeking perfection to celebrating consistent progress?

Website, links, projects & contact available on pages 205-214

CHAPTER 7: KEGAN "SMURF" GILL
DEFYING IMPOSSIBLE ODDS AND COMING OUT ON TOP

INTRODUCTION

Kegan Gill, known by his call sign "Smurf," is a former U.S. Navy F-18 Super Hornet pilot who has overcome incredible adversity. His story is one of resilience, perseverance and survival, defying all expectations after enduring a near-fatal ejection at nearly the speed of sound. This chapter delves into Kegan's extraordinary journey, the horrific accident that changed his life and the mental toughness that helped him overcome unimaginable physical and emotional challenges.

EPISODE SUMMARY

Kegan's passion for flying began at a young age, inspired by an early flight in a Cessna 152. His love for the skies led him to earn various pilot certifications, eventually becoming a flight instructor and corporate pilot. However, Kegan's real ambition was to become a Navy fighter pilot and after a lot of research and preparation, he applied for the Navy's flight programme and was accepted. This decision set him on a path to fly the F-18 Super Hornet, the same aircraft famously featured in *Top Gun: Maverick*.

Kegan's career was thriving until January 15, 2014, when disaster struck. During a training mission, Kegan was flying a routine dogfighting drill when a malfunction caused his aircraft to dive uncontrollably towards the ocean. Forced to eject at a speed of 604 knots—95% of the speed of sound—he endured catastrophic injuries. Both of his arms, legs and his neck were broken and he suffered severe nerve damage and hypothermia as he bobbed in the freezing Atlantic Ocean for over an hour before being rescued.

Despite the grim prognosis—told he might never walk again, let alone fly—Kegan fought through months of painful rehabilitation and against all odds, he eventually returned to flying. However, the physical and emotional toll continued, exacerbated by the side effects of medication and the onset of post-traumatic stress disorder (PTSD). It was through holistic approaches, including psychedelic therapy and support from various veterans' organisations, that Kegan finally found a path to healing.

Today, Kegan is an advocate for mental health, a proud husband and father and is sharing his story to inspire others to fight through adversity.

FIVE KEY LESSONS

1. Survival is a Mindset

Kegan's survival was not just due to luck but also his unyielding will to live. As he fought to stay above water in the freezing Atlantic, he relied on survival instincts and sheer determination. He believes that in any life-threatening situation, your mindset plays a crucial role in whether you make it through or give up.

My Take:

In the face of adversity, your survival depends not only on external factors but on your inner resolve. Whether it's a physical ordeal or an emotional battle, maintaining the will to push through can make the difference between success and failure.

2. Small Steps Lead to Big Results

After waking up in the hospital, paralysed and severely injured, Kegan broke down the overwhelming task of recovery into small, manageable goals. Rather than focusing on the long road ahead, he concentrated on what he could do each day—whether it was wiggling his toes or sitting up in bed.

My Take:

When faced with seemingly insurmountable challenges, break them down into smaller, achievable steps. Focusing on daily progress, no matter how small, builds momentum and leads to big results over time.

3. Resilience in the Face of Setbacks

Kegan's journey to recovery was far from linear. After returning to flying, he faced additional challenges from traumatic brain injury (TBI) and the side effects of psychotropic medications, which led to bouts of psychosis. However, he refused to let these setbacks define him and he sought alternative treatments that helped him regain control of his life.

My Take:

Resilience doesn't mean avoiding setbacks; it means refusing to be defeated by them. Life's challenges often come in waves, but by staying resilient, you can continue to move forward, even when progress feels slow.

4. Holistic Healing Can Be Life-Changing

For Kegan, traditional medical treatments weren't enough. It was only after discovering holistic therapies, including psychedelic treatments and intensive brain rehabilitation, that he began to experience meaningful recovery. These therapies helped him heal not only his body but also his mind and spirit, allowing him to reconnect with his emotions and find peace.

My Take:

Healing is not always found in conventional methods. Sometimes, exploring alternative approaches—whether they're physical, mental, or spiritual—can provide the breakthrough needed to truly recover. Don't be afraid to explore new avenues of healing, especially when traditional methods fall short.

5. The Will to Live is Paramount

One of the most powerful lessons Kegan shared was that the will to live is the ultimate survival tool. Whether fighting through hypothermia in the ocean or overcoming the darkness of suicidal thoughts, it was his strong desire to live for his family that kept him going.

My Take:

The will to live can pull you through the darkest of times. When everything feels hopeless, anchor yourself to something—your loved ones, your future, your purpose—and let that drive you to keep going.

APPLYING THE LESSONS TO LIFE

Kegan Gill's story is a testament to human resilience and the power of the mind to overcome even the most devastating challenges. Here are a few ways to apply these lessons to your own life:

- **Embrace the power of mindset:** Whether you're facing a physical challenge or emotional difficulty, your mindset can be your greatest asset. Stay focused on survival, both in the literal and metaphorical sense.

- **Break it down:** Tackle big goals by breaking them into smaller, actionable steps. Celebrate small victories, as they contribute to the overall journey.

- **Resilience over perfection:** Setbacks are inevitable, but resilience allows you to keep pushing forward, even when progress seems slow or non-existent.

- **Seek alternative paths:** Don't be afraid to explore different routes to healing or success, especially when conventional methods fail to deliver.

- **Find your "why":** In moments of despair, connect to the reasons you want to keep going. Whether it's your family, your passion, or your potential, holding on to your purpose can give you the strength to fight another day.

APPLY THE LESSONS: REFLECTION QUESTIONS

Here are some reflection questions to help you think about how to incorporate these lessons into your own life:

1. When faced with overwhelming challenges, how can you break them down into smaller, more manageable steps?

2. What are some alternative methods you could explore to improve your physical or mental well-being?

3. In what areas of your life can you strengthen your resilience and persistence?

4. What is your personal "why"—the thing that drives you to keep going when times get tough?

Website, links, projects & contact available on pages 205-214

CHAPTER 8: RICH GRAHAM
FROM NAVY SEAL TO BUILDING THE FULL SPECTRUM WARRIOR

INTRODUCTION

Rich Graham, a veteran Navy SEAL, tactical firearms instructor and nonprofit founder, takes us through his incredible journey from the rigours of SEAL training to his impactful work with Homefront K9 and Full Spectrum Warrior. In this chapter, Rich shares the mental and physical strategies that helped him succeed as a SEAL and how those lessons translate into his current mission of building resilient, self-reliant individuals and communities.

EPISODE SUMMARY

Rich's journey into the Navy SEALs began with a desire to seek challenge and purpose beyond the traditional path laid out for him. After initially pursuing architecture scholarships, Rich realised his true calling lay in serving his country and tackling the hardest challenges possible. His SEAL training included the infamous Hell Week, a gruelling trial of physical endurance and mental toughness, which he describes as his "rite of passage" to manhood.

During his six years in the SEAL Teams, Rich faced life-changing experiences, including deployment with SEAL Team 10 and later transitioning to the elite Seal Delivery Vehicle Team 2. However, a medical condition unexpectedly ended his military career. This led Rich to reinvent himself, finding new purpose as a tactical instructor and founder of Full Spectrum Warrior, where he emphasises holistic preparation—mentally, physically and tactically.

Rich also launched Homefront K9, a nonprofit providing service dogs to military families, where he discovered the transformative power of canine companions in rebuilding communication and trust within families. His story is a testament to resilience, adaptability and living a purpose-driven life.

FIVE KEY LESSONS

1. Break Challenges Into Manageable Parts

Rich emphasises breaking overwhelming tasks, like Hell Week, into smaller, more manageable goals. Focus on making it to the next meal, the next day, or the next milestone, rather than being consumed by the enormity of the challenge.

My Take:

Life's biggest challenges can feel insurmountable if faced all at once. By breaking them into smaller, actionable steps, you build momentum and stay focused on progress. This approach can be applied to any goal, from personal growth to business ventures.

2. Guard Against Negative Influences

Rich explains how maintaining a positive mental dialogue and surrounding yourself with supportive individuals is critical during stressful times. Negative influences, whether internal or external, can derail even the strongest resolve.

My Take:

Your mindset and the company you keep are critical to achieving success. Protect your mental space and seek environments that reinforce your goals. In life and business, avoid toxic people who sap your energy or plant seeds of doubt.

3. Earn Respect Daily

The SEAL ethos of "earning your Trident every day" teaches that past achievements don't guarantee future success. Rich believes that true credibility comes from continuously striving to grow, adapt and contribute value.

My Take:

Staying relevant means committing to lifelong learning and improvement. Whether in your career, relationships, or personal goals, treat every day as an opportunity to prove your worth and grow beyond yesterday's limits.

4. Lead With Purpose and Accountability

Rich highlights the importance of taking responsibility for your actions and leading with intention. He believes that adding value to others 'lives—not just your own—creates deeper meaning and motivation in any endeavour.

My Take:

Accountability fuels growth. Whether through charity, mentorship, or leadership roles, make your actions about more than just yourself. By serving others, you not only grow but also inspire those around you to do the same.

5. Failure Is a Stepping Stone to Success

Reflecting on SEAL training and sniper school, Rich notes that failure is inevitable but should always be a learning opportunity. It's not about avoiding mistakes but understanding why they happened and making necessary adjustments.

My Take:

Failure is only fatal if you let it be. Analyse your mistakes, learn from them and adjust your strategy. A growth mindset transforms setbacks into the building blocks of success.

APPLYING THE LESSONS TO LIFE

Rich's lessons from his SEAL training and his subsequent career offer a wealth of wisdom applicable to any walk of life. Here are some ways to incorporate his insights:

- **Break challenges down:** Identify the next small step you need to take toward a daunting goal. Celebrate small victories to maintain momentum.

- **Choose your influences wisely:** Audit your social circle and remove toxic influences. Surround yourself with people who inspire and support your growth.

- **Commit to daily growth:** Write down one thing you'll accomplish each day to move closer to your long-term goals.

- **Serve others:** Volunteer, mentor, or find ways to contribute to your community. Purpose is amplified when shared.

- **Reframe failure:** View setbacks as valuable lessons. Ask yourself, "What can I learn from this?" rather than dwelling on the loss.

APPLY THE LESSONS: REFLECTION QUESTIONS

- What major challenge in your life can you break into smaller, manageable goals?

- How can you surround yourself with more positive influences in your daily life?

- What is one small action you can take today to "earn your Trident" and grow?

- In what ways can you add value to someone else's life or community this week?

- Think of a recent failure: What lessons can you extract and how will you adjust your approach next time?

Website, links, projects & contact available on pages 205-214

LOUIS SKUPIEN

CHAPTER 9: MARK DIVINE
THE WARRIOR MINDSET WITH FORMER NAVY SEAL COMMANDER

INTRODUCTION

Mark Divine, a retired Navy SEAL Commander, is a master of blending the ancient art of meditation with modern-day special operations training. Mark is the founder of SEALFIT and Unbeatable Mind, where he trains elite professionals, special forces and civilians alike to master their minds, bodies and spirits. His deep insights into leadership, mental fortitude and the warrior ethos offer invaluable lessons applicable in both personal and professional life. In this chapter, we delve into Mark's journey from a small-town athlete to a Navy SEAL Commander, his transition to civilian life and the principles that guide him.

EPISODE SUMMARY

Mark's path to becoming a Navy SEAL wasn't a straight line. Raised in a small town in Upstate New York, he initially followed the traditional route of getting an MBA and working in the business world. However, an encounter with a Zen master shifted his trajectory. Meditation helped Mark realise that his true calling was to become a warrior, leading him to the SEAL Teams.

Once in the Navy SEALs, Mark excelled as a leader and trainer, integrating mental training practices, like meditation and controlled breathing, into his units. This holistic approach to training helped him and his teams remain calm under pressure and focused on the mission.

After retiring from the military, Mark transitioned to the business world, where he faced challenges adapting to civilian life. He founded SEALFIT and Unbeatable Mind, training people worldwide to adopt a warrior mindset, blending ancient philosophies with modern tactics to help individuals build mental, physical and spiritual strength.

FIVE KEY LESSONS

1. The Power of Meditation

Mark discovered meditation through a Zen master in his early 20s, which fundamentally changed his approach to life. Meditation helped him uncover his true purpose and prepared him for the challenges of SEAL training and beyond. The practice of controlling the mind allows individuals to remain calm in the face of chaos, a key to success in both combat and everyday life.

My Take:

Meditation is a powerful tool for cultivating mental resilience. By incorporating meditation into your routine, you can develop a greater sense of calm and control, enabling you to navigate life's challenges with clarity.

2. Embrace Failure as Part of Growth

Mark emphasised the Navy SEAL principle that failure is inevitable and essential for growth. Instead of fearing failure, embrace it as a learning opportunity. In the SEALs, failure is a tool for improvement, helping individuals and teams refine their tactics, skills and strategies.

My Take:

Reframing failure as a stepping stone to success can change how you approach challenges. When you stop fearing failure and start viewing it as part of the process, you open yourself up to greater learning and improvement.

3. Build a Strong Team with Aligned Values

Mark highlighted how the SEAL Teams operate with a deep sense of trust and unity. In the military, teams succeed because they share a common mission and values. In the business world, however, this alignment can be harder to achieve. It takes intentional effort to build a team that shares a vision and works cohesively toward a common goal.

My Take:

The strength of any team lies in its ability to align around shared values and vision. Whether in business or personal life, take time to foster a culture of trust and shared purpose within your team to ensure success.

4. Feed the Wolf of Courage

Drawing inspiration from an ancient Native American story, Mark explained how every person has two wolves inside them—the wolf of fear and the wolf of courage. The one that wins is the one you feed. By focusing on positivity, gratitude and courage, you can starve fear and live a more courageous and fulfilled life.

My Take:

Your mindset shapes your reality. By feeding the wolf of courage, you cultivate a positive, resilient and fearless attitude, enabling you to face challenges head-on and live with purpose.

5. Continuous Training and Evolution

In the SEAL Teams, training is a constant part of life. Mark stressed the importance of maintaining a mindset of continual growth, whether you're on the battlefield or in the boardroom. In an ever-changing world, staying stagnant is not an option. You must continuously evolve, train and improve to remain effective and relevant.

My Take:

Success is a journey, not a destination. By committing to lifelong learning and self-improvement, you position yourself to thrive in any environment, no matter how volatile or uncertain.

APPLYING THE LESSONS TO LIFE

Mark Divine's teachings are a roadmap for anyone looking to cultivate mental toughness, lead with integrity and achieve greatness. Here are some ways to apply his principles:

- **Start meditating daily:** Even just five minutes a day can help you build mental clarity and resilience.

- **Reframe failure:** Instead of seeing setbacks as defeats, view them as valuable learning experiences that will ultimately lead to growth.

- **Focus on team alignment:** Whether you lead a business or work within a team, ensure that everyone shares the same values and vision to foster trust and collaboration.

- **Feed the right wolf:** Make conscious decisions to cultivate courage and positivity in your life, avoiding negativity and fear.

- **Never stop training:** Keep pushing yourself to learn, grow and adapt to new challenges. Success comes from continuous evolution.

APPLY THE LESSONS: REFLECTION QUESTIONS

1. How can you incorporate meditation or other mental training practices into your daily routine to improve focus and resilience?

2. What failures in your life can you reframe as learning opportunities and how can you use them to move forward?

3. Is your team aligned around shared values and a common vision? If not, what steps can you take to create that alignment?

4. Are you feeding the wolf of courage or fear? How can you starve fear and cultivate more courage in your life?

5. What areas of your life could benefit from continuous training and improvement?

Website, links, projects & contact available on pages 205-214

CHAPTER 10: TAYLOR "FEMA" HIESTER
TEAM BUILDING MASTERY

INTRODUCTION

In this episode of Talk4, I had the privilege of speaking with Taylor "Fema" Hiester, a highly skilled F-16 Viper Demo Team pilot. Taylor's passion for aviation, his journey into the U.S. Air Force and his commitment to inspiring others through his role in the demonstration team made this conversation deeply impactful. Taylor shared his story of growing up in Pennsylvania, his love for aviation from a young age and his remarkable career path, leading him to one of the most iconic fighter jets in the world—the F-16. Through our discussion, we uncovered valuable lessons about dedication, perseverance and leadership that can resonate with anyone chasing their own dreams. Let's dive in.

EPISODE SUMMARY

Taylor "Fema" Hiester grew up in a small town in Pennsylvania, where his passion for aviation took flight at a young age. He vividly recalls the moment that sparked his desire to become a fighter pilot—the events of September 11th, 2001. Witnessing the fighter jets soaring over New York left a lasting impression on him, solidifying his goal to protect his country while flying fast jets. Taylor pursued this dream by joining the Air Force ROTC at Penn State and eventually earned his way into the elite ranks of fighter pilots, flying the F-16.

Throughout our conversation, Taylor emphasised the importance of controlling the control-ables in life and how sheer determination, paired with timing and a bit of luck, led him to his dream role. He also spoke passionately about the unique qualities of the F-16, describing it as the perfect jet for a solo pilot. Taylor's role as a demonstration pilot isn't just about flying; it's about inspiring the next generation and reminding people of the importance of serving their communities. His dedication to this mission is clear in every aspect of his leadership within the team, which he likens to a family.

Taylor's journey, insights and experiences provide powerful lessons that can be applied both to life and to any professional pursuit.

FIVE KEY LESSONS

1. Passion Can Be Ignited at a Young Age

Taylor's aviation journey started as a child, with his mother encouraging him to explore flying at a local airport. From flying his first plane at age nine, Taylor never let go of that passion.

My Take:

It's important to pay attention to the interests that light you up early in life. These moments of inspiration can often lead to lifelong pursuits.

2. Control the Controllables

Taylor believes that success is a combination of ability, preparation and luck. By focusing on what you can control—your effort, your choices—you increase the likelihood that you'll be in the right place at the right time.

My Take:

In both personal and professional life, many variables are out of our control. But by focusing on the things we *can* control, like preparation and discipline, we create more opportunities for success.

3. Find Joy in Responsibility

Taylor spoke about the satisfaction that comes from being the sole pilot in the F-16, where every decision in the cockpit rests on his shoulders. This responsibility drives him to excel and keeps him sharp.

My Take:

Embracing responsibility can lead to personal growth. Instead of shying away from challenges, take pride in carrying the weight of your goals. This mindset helps you develop leadership qualities and accountability.

4. Small Teams Can Achieve Big Things

Taylor described the F-16 Viper Demo Team as a close-knit family where everyone plays a critical role. Leading a small team means there's no anonymity—everyone's contributions matter deeply.

My Take:

In any team, be it in business or personal projects, building strong relationships and recognising the value of each member creates a culture of trust and high performance.

5. Inspiration Is Part of the Mission

Beyond the technical skill required to fly the F-16, Taylor emphasised that a key part of his job is inspiring Americans to serve their communities. Whether through school visits or air shows, the impact his team has goes beyond the airstrip.

My Take:

Whatever your career or passion, consider how you can use it to inspire and uplift others. By thinking beyond personal achievements, we contribute positively to the lives of those around us.

APPLYING THE LESSONS TO LIFE

The lessons from Taylor's story aren't just for aspiring fighter pilots—they can be applied to any goal you may be pursuing. Here are some key ways to integrate these lessons into your life:

- Nurture your passions: Whether you're 9 or 99, it's never too late to pursue the things that bring you joy. Reflect on the moments when you've felt the most alive and consider how you can incorporate more of that into your life.

- Focus on what you can control: Rather than worrying about what's out of your hands, invest your energy into what you can influence. Whether it's your work ethic, your preparation, or your attitude, controlling these factors will help you reach your goals more effectively.

- Embrace responsibility: Don't shy away from taking charge in your personal or professional life. By stepping up, you not only grow but also earn the respect of those around you.

- Value your team: A small, dedicated group of people can accomplish incredible things when everyone feels valued. Whether you're leading a team or are part of one, contribute to a culture of trust and support.

- Inspire others: Your achievements can serve as motivation for others. Whether through direct mentorship or leading by example, find ways to inspire the people around you to pursue their own dreams.

APPLY THE LESSONS: REFLECTION QUESTIONS

- What passions from your early years are still a part of you today? How can you reconnect with them to fuel your current pursuits?

- Are there areas in your life where you could better focus on the controllables? How can you shift your mindset to emphasise what's within your influence?

- In what ways could you take on more responsibility in your life or career? What benefits might come from stepping up?

- Think about the teams you're part of. How can you contribute more to the overall success and cohesion of the group?

- How can you inspire someone in your community or field with the work you're doing right now?

Website, links, projects & contact available on pages 205-214

CHAPTER 11: TUCKER "CINCO" HAMILTON
AN AI INSIGHT FROM THE U.S.A.F

INTRODUCTION

Col (Ret) Tucker "Cinco" Hamilton is a distinguished fighter pilot and test pilot for the United States Air Force, overseeing developmental flight tests for multiple airframes, including the F-15C, F-15E and F-15EX. Currently, he served in dual roles as the former Operations Group Commander of the 96th Test Wing at Eglin Air Force Base and as Chief of AI Test and Operations for the Department of the Air Force. Tucker's expertise spans cutting-edge technologies like autonomous aircraft and AI-powered capabilities. In this chapter, we explore Tucker's path from a high school dropout to a decorated fighter pilot and commander, along with his insights on AI's potential in aviation and beyond.

EPISODE SUMMARY

Tucker's journey to becoming a fighter pilot was unconventional. Dropping out of high school, he eventually enrolled in the Air Force ROTC at the University of Colorado, inspired by movies like *Saving Private Ryan* and *Braveheart* and his parents' careers as firefighters. He didn't initially plan to become a pilot due to failing the depth perception test, but later passed, securing his place in flight school.

His career took him from Navy pilot training to flying fighter jets for the Air Force, where he found his passion for military aviation. Over time, Tucker became a test pilot, overseeing the development and testing of various fighter aircraft and their systems. Today, he's at the forefront of integrating AI into military aviation, helping the Air Force navigate the ethical and operational challenges of autonomous aircraft.

A pivotal moment in Tucker's career was his involvement in the development of the F-35 fighter jet. This opened his eyes to the technological advancements that could revolutionise air combat and military strategy. He's now heavily involved in shaping AI policy, ensuring that its implementation remains ethical and effective across military and civilian sectors.

FIVE KEY LESSONS

1. Unconventional Paths Can Lead to Success

Tucker's path to becoming a fighter pilot was anything but typical. He initially dropped out of high school and had no plans to join the military, but a chance encounter with the Air Force ROTC at his university changed everything. His story is a testament to the idea that success can come from unexpected directions if you remain open to new opportunities.

My Take:

Life's path is rarely linear. Being open to unexpected opportunities and taking calculated risks can lead to rewarding outcomes, even if your journey doesn't start off as planned.

2. The Power of AI in Aviation

As a test pilot, Tucker is deeply involved in the integration of AI into military aviation. AI is revolutionising how aircraft operate, from autonomous drones to AI-powered decision-making systems in cockpits. These advancements offer enormous potential but also require careful ethical considerations to ensure they are used responsibly.

My Take:

The future of technology, especially in fields like aviation, lies in the balance between human oversight and AI-driven capabilities. Learning how to integrate and regulate AI will be crucial in the years ahead.

3. Failures are Part of Growth

Tucker's story includes moments of doubt, such as when he nearly quit Navy pilot training. However, these moments of struggle ultimately made him a stronger, more determined individual. His persistence, supported by his wife's encouragement, allowed him to overcome challenges and excel in his career.

My Take:

Failure is not the end—it's an opportunity to learn and grow. By pushing through difficult times, we often discover strength we didn't know we had, leading to personal and professional growth.

4. Ethics and Responsibility in AI Development

One of Tucker's primary roles is ensuring the ethical use of AI in the Air Force. He stresses the importance of creating safeguards to prevent misuse of AI technology. Without these ethical guidelines, AI could pose risks to society, particularly if rushed or developed carelessly.

My Take:

As AI becomes more integrated into our daily lives, it's essential to prioritise ethics and responsibility in its development. Thoughtful, deliberate progress is key to ensuring AI serves humanity in positive and productive ways.

5. Service as a Core Value

Tucker's dedication to service extends beyond his military career. He believes that everyone has a role to play in serving their community and country, whether through military service, volunteering, or simply helping those around them. Service brings perspective and purpose to life.

My Take:

Serving others, whether on a large or small scale, gives life meaning. Whether through career or personal acts of kindness, service can help bridge divides and create stronger communities.

APPLYING THE LESSONS TO LIFE

Tucker "Cinco" Hamilton's story offers valuable insights for anyone seeking to blend personal ambition with ethical responsibility. Here are a few ways to apply his lessons:

- Be open to unconventional opportunities, as success can come from unexpected directions.

- Embrace AI and technological advancements, but remain vigilant about their ethical use.

- Learn from failures rather than letting them deter you from your goals.

- Strive to serve others, whether through your career or personal actions, as service brings perspective and fulfilment.

- Stay committed to learning and adapting, especially as technology continues to evolve.

APPLY THE LESSONS: REFLECTION QUESTIONS

- How can you remain open to unconventional paths in your life or career?

- What steps can you take to better understand the ethical implications of AI in your field?

- Are there any recent failures you can reframe as opportunities for growth?

- How can you serve your community or those around you in meaningful ways?

- How can you stay informed and adaptable in the face of rapid technological advancements?

Website, links, projects & contact available on pages 205-214

CHAPTER 12: TYLER GREY
THE PURSUIT OF PASSION WILL MAKE YOU A WINNER

INTRODUCTION

Tyler Grey, a former U.S. Army Special Operations soldier, has an extraordinary story of resilience, transition and finding new purpose in the entertainment industry. After serving nearly a decade in Special Operations, Tyler was medically retired due to injuries sustained in combat, leading him to a new career as a bodyguard and later in Hollywood, where he now stars in and works behind the scenes on the hit show *SEAL Team*. His journey offers deep insights into the mindset required to overcome adversity, rebuild oneself and thrive in a new, challenging environment. In this chapter, we explore Tyler's military career, his foray into the entertainment world and the lessons he's learned along the way.

EPISODE SUMMARY

Tyler's path into the military wasn't a decision he made lightly—it was something he felt he was born to do. From a young age, he was fascinated with war and the military and by the time he was old enough, enlisting felt like his natural calling. His passion drove him to ask the Army recruitment office for the toughest challenge they had, leading him to the Army Rangers. Tyler's career in Special Operations spanned nearly a decade and included multiple combat deployments. However, his military career was cut short after he was severely injured by an IED.

Transitioning out of the military was challenging. Tyler spent several years working as a bodyguard while trying to find his place in the entertainment industry. His big break came when he was hired as a military advisor for *SEAL Team*, a role that eventually led to him acting and directing episodes of the show. Despite the physical and mental toll of his injuries, Tyler found new purpose in sharing authentic military stories on screen, using his personal experience to influence how military characters are portrayed.

Tyler's resilience, determination and ability to adapt to new challenges are evident throughout his journey. His story is a testament to how adversity can serve as a catalyst for growth and new opportunities.

FIVE KEY LESSONS

1. Follow Your Passion Relentlessly

From an early age, Tyler knew he wanted to join the military. His decision to pursue Special Operations was driven by a deep-seated passion for the challenge, not external pressures. His story illustrates how pursuing what you are truly passionate about, even in the face of adversity, leads to a more fulfilling life.

My Take:

Passion is an unstoppable force. When you pursue what you genuinely love, no obstacle feels too big and the rewards become intrinsic. Follow your passion and the rest will fall into place.

2. Embrace the Toughest Challenges

Tyler's military journey began with a challenge—he specifically asked the recruitment office for the toughest contract available. His desire to be pushed to his limits was key to his growth and success in Special Operations. This mentality of seeking out and embracing difficult situations has carried over into his post-military life.

My Take:

Growth comes from discomfort. Actively seek out the hardest challenges in your life, knowing that they will sharpen your skills and character. Embrace the discomfort; it's where true progress happens.

3. Resilience Comes from Doing What You Love

Tyler learned early on that passion drives resilience. Despite the hardships of military training and later, the injuries he sustained, his passion for the job kept him going. Similarly, his love for storytelling helped him navigate the tough transition into Hollywood.

My Take:

Resilience is rooted in passion. When you're deeply connected to what you do, you find the strength to push through setbacks.

Make sure you're on the path that resonates with who you are at your core.

4. Align Your Effort with Your True Self

Tyler emphasised the importance of following your innate interests rather than being swayed by societal expectations. He believes that people succeed when their efforts are aligned with their true passions, rather than conforming to what others think they should do.

My Take:

Authenticity is powerful. Aligning your actions with your true self not only enhances your ability to succeed but also brings deeper satisfaction. Take time to reflect on who you really are and what you genuinely want from life.

5. Every Adversity is Temporary

Having been severely injured and forced to leave the military, Tyler knows firsthand how devastating setbacks can be. However, he also understands that adversity is temporary and the growth that comes from it often leads to something better in the long run.

My Take:

Tough times don't last, but the lessons they teach can have a lasting impact. Every difficult moment is an opportunity to grow and will one day be something you look back on with gratitude for the strength it gave you.

APPLYING THE LESSONS TO LIFE

Tyler Grey's story offers a powerful reminder that passion, resilience and authenticity are key to overcoming life's challenges. Here are some ways to apply his principles:

- Follow your passion: Identify what you are truly passionate about and relentlessly pursue it.

- Embrace discomfort: Take on the toughest challenges, knowing that they will make you stronger.

- Align your effort: Make sure the work you do resonates with your true self, not just societal expectations.

- Be resilient: Remember that adversity is temporary and every setback is a chance to grow.

- Stay authentic: Don't let others dictate your path— follow the direction that feels most natural to you.

APPLY THE LESSONS: REFLECTION QUESTIONS

- What are you truly passionate about and how can you incorporate that into your daily life?

- What challenges have you been avoiding and how can you confront them head-on?

- Are your efforts aligned with your authentic self, or are you following external pressures?

- How can you cultivate resilience during tough times?

- What past adversities have led to positive growth and how can you use that perspective in the future?

Website, links, projects & contact available on pages 205-214

CHAPTER 13: ERIC LEE
WHAT WE CAN LEARN FROM WHAT'S HAPPENED IN THE MUSIC INDUSTRY

INTRODUCTION

Eric Lee is a rising star in the country music scene, blending heartfelt lyrics with masterful production. Hailing from South Florida, Eric's journey into the world of music production and songwriting has been filled with dedication, passion and a willingness to adapt to the ever-changing landscape of the music industry. In this chapter, we explore his journey from a producer to a country music artist and how his experiences in music licensing and personal perseverance have shaped his career.

EPISODE SUMMARY

Eric's musical story began in South Florida, where he was raised by his grandmother, who played a crucial role in fostering his passion for music. Starting with guitar lessons, Eric quickly formed bands and honed his craft. His journey took a pivotal turn when he attended audio engineering school, which opened doors for him to pursue music production professionally. After producing multiple records, he found a niche in music licensing, co-writing a song that was featured in a Toyota Super Bowl commercial and the Winter Olympics.

The pandemic shifted Eric's focus from producing for others to releasing his own music. His debut single, *Same Dirt Road*, was a breakthrough, resonating with listeners due to its message of unity during a time of global division. The song received massive support, getting featured on editorial playlists by Spotify Nashville and even being played on country music radio stations. Eric's story is one of adapting, learning and continuing to push the boundaries of his creativity.

FIVE KEY LESSONS

1. The Power of Music Licensing

Eric highlights the importance of music licensing as a financial lifeline for artists. Licensing allows musicians to retain their rights while earning income from their work. This was a game-changer for Eric and his advice to other musicians is to explore music pitching companies to find opportunities in TV, film and advertisements.

My Take:

Music licensing is a great avenue for artists looking to monetise their creations beyond streaming platforms. It allows musicians to keep ownership while opening new doors for exposure and income.

2. Embrace the Unpredictability of the Music Industry

Eric entered the world of music as a producer and transitioned to an artist during the pandemic. His journey was full of unexpected opportunities, showing that flexibility is key in the music industry. Staying open to new paths can lead to success in unexpected ways.

My Take:

Adaptability is crucial in today's fast-paced world. Whether in music or any other field, being willing to pivot when needed can lead to unexpected opportunities and growth.

3. Collaboration Opens Doors

One of the highlights of Eric's career was working with Vince Powell, an industry-renowned mixing engineer. Reaching out to Vince helped Eric elevate his debut single, showcasing the power of collaboration in bringing ideas to life.

My Take:

Collaboration can accelerate progress. Don't be afraid to reach out to industry experts or like-minded professionals. You never know who might respond and what magic can come from working together.

4. Stay Ahead of Technology

The music industry is in constant flux and Eric emphasises the importance of staying informed about new trends, like AI in music and the evolving nature of social media algorithms. His insight into how Spotify and social media work today shows the need to constantly evolve your strategy as a musician.

My Take:

Continuous learning is key to staying relevant. Keeping up with technological advancements and trends allows you to stay competitive and make informed decisions about your career.

5. The Importance of a Strong Message

Eric's song *Same Dirt Road* was successful partly because it carried a message of unity during a time of global division. The song resonated with listeners because it tapped into the collective sentiment of togetherness, making it stand out in a crowded marketplace.

My Take:

The message behind your work matters. Whether it's a song, a business, or a creative project, connecting with your audience on a deeper level through a meaningful message can amplify its impact.

APPLYING THE LESSONS TO LIFE

Eric Lee's insights can be applied to anyone striving for success in a creative field. Here's how you can take these lessons and make them your own:

- Explore alternative revenue streams: Look into licensing opportunities or other avenues to diversify your income.

- Embrace unpredictability: Stay open to new paths and opportunities, even if they weren't part of your original plan.

- Collaborate: Don't hesitate to reach out to others in your field for advice, mentorship, or collaboration.

- Stay informed: Keep up with the latest trends and technologies in your industry to stay ahead of the curve.

- Create with purpose: Whether through music, writing, or any creative endeavour, ensure your message is clear and resonates with your audience.

APPLY THE LESSONS: REFLECTION QUESTIONS

- How can you explore new income opportunities in your field, similar to Eric's approach to music licensing?

- In what areas of your life could you benefit from being more flexible and adaptable?

- Who in your industry could you collaborate with to bring your ideas to life?

- What new technology or trends should you learn more about to stay competitive in your field?

- Does your work carry a message that resonates with others? How can you refine that message to connect more deeply with your audience?

Website, links, projects & contact available on pages 205-214

LOUIS SKUPIEN

CHAPTER 14: ANTHONY SMITH
MASTERING THE ART OF VIDEO STORYTELLING

INTRODUCTION

Anthony Smith, the Director of Trailers for the successful "Diary of a CEO" podcast, has played an instrumental role in elevating the show's presence with his emotionally engaging and cinematic trailers. With a background in film production and social media marketing, Anthony's unique approach to storytelling through video has set new standards in podcast promotion. In this chapter, we'll explore Anthony's journey from aspiring actor to film editor, how he overcame challenges along the way and the key principles that drive his creative process.

EPISODE SUMMARY

Anthony's path into video production started in an unexpected way. Originally aspiring to be an actor, he quickly realised that his passion lay behind the camera. After experiencing stage fright during his GCSEs, he turned his attention to film production. His fascination with behind-the-scenes featurettes and the craft of filmmaking led him to study Film Production at university, where his ambition shifted to becoming a director.

After university, Anthony co-founded a video production company with a friend, starting from scratch with no loans or outside funding. Over time, he discovered his passion for editing, eventually leading to a role as a senior editor for a social media marketing agency. His clients included major names like Disney, Marvel and James Bond. It was through these experiences that Anthony honed his skills in storytelling and crafting emotional narratives.

Anthony's journey culminated in his role with "Diary of a CEO," where he is responsible for creating compelling trailers that encapsulate the essence of the podcast's most dramatic and emotional moments. His approach to marketing through video has redefined how podcasts are promoted, combining the power of storytelling with the visual techniques of cinema.

FIVE KEY LESSONS

1. The Power of Storytelling in Video

For Anthony, storytelling is at the heart of every successful trailer. By crafting a narrative that takes viewers on an emotional journey, he ensures that each trailer leaves a lasting impact. Whether it's joy, sadness, or inspiration, the emotions evoked through storytelling drive engagement and compel audiences to watch the full episode.

My Take:

Effective storytelling is key to capturing and retaining attention. Focus on creating narratives that resonate emotionally with your audience and you'll find them more invested in your content.

2. Embrace Feedback and Adapt

Anthony's career taught him the value of feedback in the creative process. Early in his career, he realised that meeting client expectations while feeding his creative side was crucial. Balancing both requires adaptability and openness to feedback.

My Take:

Learning to adapt and accept constructive criticism is essential for growth. Seek feedback from others and use it to fine-tune your work to meet both creative and practical goals.

3. The Importance of Crafting a Niche

In a competitive industry, Anthony emphasises the importance of finding your unique voice. His success at "Diary of a CEO" is attributed to the show's ability to tap into its niche—Steve Bartlett's skill at drawing out raw emotion from guests and the trailers that reflect this emotional depth.

My Take:

Discovering your niche is crucial for standing out. Focus on what makes your content different and lean into it to build a loyal audience.

4. Continuous Learning and Evolution

Despite his success, Anthony is constantly looking for ways to improve. Whether it's mastering new techniques in editing or experimenting with 3D motion graphics, his commitment to evolving his craft keeps his work fresh and engaging.

My Take:

Never stop learning. The more you push yourself to grow, the more you'll be able to offer creatively. Continuous evolution is what keeps you at the top of your game.

5. The Future is Visual

Anthony highlights the growing importance of video in podcasting. With platforms like YouTube and Spotify offering video formats, visual content is becoming a crucial part of audience engagement. By incorporating video into your podcasting strategy, you tap into a new demographic of viewers who prefer watching over listening.

My Take:

Incorporating video content is no longer optional—it's the future of podcasting. If you haven't already, consider adding video to your podcasting toolkit to reach a broader audience.

APPLYING THE LESSONS TO LIFE

Anthony's approach to video storytelling and marketing offers valuable insights for anyone looking to enhance their creative and promotional efforts. Here's how you can apply his lessons:

- Focus on storytelling: Whether you're producing videos or writing, always centre your work around a compelling narrative that evokes emotion.
- Embrace feedback: Don't shy away from constructive criticism—it's your best tool for improvement.

- Find your niche: Identify what makes your content unique and use that to build a strong, loyal audience.

- Keep learning: Stay curious and continuously push the boundaries of your skills.

- Use video: Leverage the power of visual content to engage your audience on multiple platforms.

APPLY THE LESSONS: REFLECTION QUESTIONS

- How can you incorporate more storytelling elements into your content to make it more engaging?

- What steps can you take to seek feedback and use it to improve your work?

- What is your unique niche and how can you capitalise on it to stand out in your field?

- What new skills or techniques can you learn to keep evolving in your craft?

- How can you integrate video into your podcast or content strategy to engage a wider audience?

Website, links, projects & contact available on pages 205-214

LOUIS SKUPIEN

CHAPTER 15: KIRK LIPPOLD
WHEN TRUE LEADERSHIP IS TESTED

INTRODUCTION

Kirk Lippold, a retired U.S. Navy Commander, is best known for his leadership during the 2000 terrorist attack on the USS Cole. As the commanding officer of the Cole, Lippold faced one of the most devastating attacks on a U.S. Navy warship in modern history. His response to the crisis and the lessons he learned have made him a respected figure in leadership, crisis management and military circles. In this chapter, we explore Kirk's naval career, his experience commanding the USS Cole during the attack and the leadership principles he applied under extreme pressure.

EPISODE SUMMARY

Kirk Lippold's naval career began when he entered the U.S. Naval Academy in 1977. Over the next two decades, he followed a traditional path in surface warfare, serving on multiple ships and advancing through the ranks. His career culminated in being appointed as the commanding officer of the USS Cole, an Arleigh Burke-class destroyer, in 1999. His leadership style emphasised accountability, professional competence and continuous improvement, pushing his crew to meet higher standards every day.

On October 12, 2000, while refuelling in the port of Aden, Yemen, the USS Cole was attacked by Al-Qaeda terrorists using a boat loaded with explosives. The explosion ripped a 40-foot hole in the side of the ship, killing 17 sailors and injuring 37 others. Despite the chaos, Kirk remained calm and decisive, rallying his crew to save the ship and evacuate the wounded. His leadership during and after the attack became a case study in crisis management, with lasting effects on naval operations and security protocols.

In the aftermath, Kirk focused on maintaining morale and unity among his crew. He has continued to share his experiences through speaking engagements, encouraging others to lead with integrity and resilience in the face of adversity.

FIVE KEY LESSONS

1. Accountability at All Levels

Kirk instilled in his crew that every individual was responsible for their actions and the consequences that followed. His philosophy was that leaders must first provide their teams with the training, tools and time to perform their duties well. Once equipped, the crew was expected to uphold the highest standards and be accountable for their performance, fostering a culture of professionalism.

My Take:

Accountability is foundational to strong leadership. By holding yourself and others responsible, you create an environment where growth and success become possible.

2. Calmness Under Pressure

During the attack, Kirk knew that if he showed panic, it would spread rapidly through the crew. He made a conscious decision to remain calm and composed, understanding that his crew needed to see confidence from their leader. This helped maintain order, focus on damage control and prevent further chaos amidst the devastation.

My Take:

Staying calm in a crisis is critical. Your demeanour sets the tone for those around you, allowing your team to respond effectively and efficiently, even under pressure.

3. Trust in Your Team

One of Kirk's key leadership principles was to trust his team to perform their duties without micromanaging. After the explosion, the crew fell back on their training and responded exactly as they had been prepared to—dividing into teams focused on damage control, security and medical assistance.

My Take:

Trust empowers people to rise to the occasion. When you trust your team to do their job, they will not only meet expectations but often exceed them in critical moments.

4. Lead with Integrity

Kirk emphasises the importance of integrity in leadership, defining it as the ability to make the right moral and ethical decisions, regardless of the consequences. During and after the attack, he was faced with difficult choices, but his commitment to integrity guided him in doing what was right for his crew and his mission.

My Take:

Integrity is non-negotiable. Leaders who act with integrity build trust and inspire those around them, especially when the stakes are high.

5. Prepare for the Unexpected

The attack on the USS Cole was a stark reminder that even in routine situations, unexpected events can occur. Kirk's leadership underlined the importance of preparation—through training, contingency planning and fostering resilience within his team.

My Take:

Preparation is key to handling unforeseen challenges. Always be ready for the unexpected and build a team that is trained to adapt and respond swiftly when situations change.

APPLYING THE LESSONS TO LIFE

Kirk Lippold's leadership during the USS Cole attack offers valuable lessons for leaders in all fields. Here are some ways to apply his principles in your own life:

- Take responsibility for your actions and decisions. Own the outcomes and use them as opportunities for learning and growth.

- Practice staying calm under pressure. When faced with adversity, take a moment to breathe, assess the situation and lead with a steady hand.

- Trust your team. Provide them with the necessary tools and training, then step back and let them excel.

- Always lead with integrity. Make decisions that align with your values, even when it's difficult.

- Prepare for the unexpected by fostering a culture of readiness and resilience within your team.

APPLY THE LESSONS: REFLECTION QUESTIONS

- How can you practice accountability in your daily life and ensure you follow through on your commitments?

- What techniques can you use to remain calm and composed during stressful situations?

- How can you build trust with your team or those around you?

- Are there areas of your life where you could lead with greater integrity? What steps can you take to strengthen your moral compass?

- How prepared are you for unexpected challenges and what can you do to increase your readiness?

Website, links, projects & contact available on pages 205-214

CHAPTER 16: TIM PARLATORE
THE ETHICS OF LAW & BASIC SELF PROTECTION

INTRODUCTION

Tim Parlatore is a renowned lawyer and managing partner at Parlatore Law Group, specialising in high-stakes litigation and criminal defence. His legal prowess has made him a key figure in some of the most publicised cases in recent years, including work for high-profile clients such as former President Donald Trump and Navy SEAL Eddie Gallagher. In this chapter, we delve into Tim's journey from a Navy officer to a lawyer, his views on legal ethics and the importance of defending constitutional rights, no matter the client.

EPISODE SUMMARY

Tim Parlatore's career started in the U.S. Navy, where he served as a Surface Warfare Officer after graduating from the U.S. Naval Academy. His decision to pursue law came after helping a close friend navigate a disciplinary issue while still in the Navy, igniting a passion for defending others. This led him to

Brooklyn Law School and, eventually, a thriving career in high-stakes criminal defence and civil litigation.

Tim's legal journey has been defined by his dedication to protecting the rights of individuals, even those whom society may deem unsympathetic. His work includes defending clients involved in organised crime, high-profile politicians and others entangled in contentious legal battles. Despite receiving death threats and facing public scrutiny, Tim emphasises that his role as a lawyer is to ensure the government respects the Constitution, regardless of the public's perception of his clients.

Parlatore's approach to law blends his military discipline with a sharp legal mind, enabling him to navigate complex legal waters and protect his clients' rights. His story is not just about high-profile cases but about the importance of upholding the legal system's integrity in the face of public and political pressure.

FIVE KEY LESSONS

1. Upholding Constitutional Rights

Tim's approach to law is rooted in ensuring that the government respects the Constitution, regardless of who the client is. Whether defending notorious criminals or politicians, he insists that everyone is entitled to a fair trial and that constitutional rights are inviolable.

My Take:

Protecting individual rights is paramount in any legal system. It reminds us that justice must be blind to prejudice and favouritism, ensuring fair treatment for all, no matter how unpopular they might be.

2. Ethics Above Personal Bias

Throughout his career, Tim has represented clients from all sides of the political spectrum. His ethical compass guides him to separate personal beliefs from professional duties. He explains that defending someone's rights doesn't imply endorsing their actions or beliefs.

My Take:

In our personal and professional lives, it's crucial to maintain integrity and keep personal emotions separate from duty. This balance allows for objective decision-making and fairness.

3. Dealing with Public and Media Pressure

Tim frequently works in the limelight, with cases that attract public and media scrutiny. He advises that the key to handling this is focusing on the facts and not being swayed by public opinion. Tim makes it clear that news reports are often influenced by bias and the truth is often far more nuanced than what's presented in the media.

My Take:

In a world dominated by media narratives, it's essential to remain focused on facts and not allow external pressures to dictate our actions. This applies not only in legal battles but in everyday decision-making.

4. Adversity as a Teacher

From his military service to his legal career, Tim learned that adversity is the greatest teacher. Overcoming challenges and hardships has been central to his growth and success, both personally and professionally.

My Take:

Adversity shapes character. Embracing difficult situations as learning experiences can lead to immense personal and professional growth.

5. The Importance of Preparation

In the courtroom, Tim emphasises the importance of thorough preparation. Understanding every detail of a case, from the evidence to the legal technicalities, is crucial for mounting a successful defence.

My Take:

Whether in law, business, or life, preparation is key. Being well-prepared can give you the confidence to face challenges head-on and improve your chances of success.

APPLYING THE LESSONS TO LIFE

Tim Parlatore's experiences offer valuable lessons not just for legal professionals, but for anyone navigating complex or challenging situations. Here are a few ways to apply his principles:

- **Defend your rights:** Understand your legal rights and stand up for them in all aspects of life.

- **Separate personal feelings from professional responsibilities:** In your career, focus on the task at hand without letting emotions cloud your judgment.

- **Prepare thoroughly for challenges:** Whether it's a job interview, a project, or a personal challenge, preparation is the foundation of success.

- **Embrace adversity:** Instead of shying away from difficulties, view them as opportunities for growth.

- **Stay grounded in facts:** Avoid being swayed by public opinion or media narratives; focus on facts and make informed decisions.

APPLY THE LESSONS: REFLECTION QUESTIONS

- How do you handle external pressures, whether from media, peers, or public opinion?

- What strategies can you implement to better prepare yourself for challenges in your personal and professional life?

- How do you ensure that you remain ethical and fair in situations where your personal feelings may conflict with your responsibilities?

- Are there any rights or legal protections you're not fully aware of in your personal or professional life? How can you become more informed?

- How can adversity in your current circumstances be turned into a learning opportunity?

Website, links, projects & contact available on pages 205-214

CHAPTER 17: SAMUEL "RAZZ" LARSON
FLYING THE USA'S BEST KEPT MILITARY SECRET

INTRODUCTION

Captain Samuel "RaZZ" Larson is a highly experienced F-22 Raptor pilot and the Commander of the F-22 Demonstration Team for the 2023-2024 air show seasons. RaZZ has dedicated his career to flying one of the most advanced fighter jets in the world and now leads a team that inspires audiences across the globe with their breathtaking displays. In this chapter, we'll explore RaZZ's journey into aviation, his experiences flying the F-22 and the profound lessons he's learned as a pilot and leader.

EPISODE SUMMARY

Samuel Larson, better known as RaZZ, grew up attending air shows, which sparked his interest in aviation from a young age. He pursued this passion through high school, taking photos for an aviation magazine and eventually found himself at the U.S. Air Force Academy. There, he honed his skills, setting his sights on becoming a fighter pilot and ultimately achieving his goal of flying the F-22 Raptor.

His career has taken him through rigorous training, including his selection as an instructor pilot and eventually becoming the Commander of the F-22 Demonstration Team. His journey to becoming an F-22 pilot was marked by persistence, dedication and a focus on excellence.

Throughout the episode, RaZZ discussed the challenges and rewards of flying the F-22, including the intense physical demands of pulling high G-forces and the thrill of demonstrating the jet's capabilities at air shows. His experiences highlight the importance of preparation, teamwork and mental fortitude in both military aviation and everyday life.

FIVE KEY LESSONS

1. Preparation and Visualisation are Key

RaZZ emphasised the importance of thorough preparation and visualisation in his work. Whether it's a combat mission or a demonstration flight, his success begins with careful mission planning and mentally rehearsing every aspect of the flight. This process helps him stay proactive rather than reactive when challenges arise.

My Take:

Visualisation can be a powerful tool in any field. Whether preparing for a presentation, a competition, or an important task, mentally walking through the process beforehand can help you stay focused and perform better under pressure.

2. Teamwork Builds Success

Although the F-22 demonstration flights focus on a single pilot, RaZZ highlighted how critical teamwork is to his success. His team of maintainers, safety observers and PR professionals work together to ensure every flight runs smoothly and each member contributes to the mission.

My Take:

Success is rarely achieved alone. Surrounding yourself with a team of dedicated individuals who share the same vision can help ensure that you meet your goals, whether in business or personal endeavours.

3. Embrace the Challenges

Flying the F-22 requires dealing with intense G-forces and demanding mental and physical preparation. RaZZ discussed how flying such a powerful jet at air shows is both exhilarating and exhausting, but those challenges are what make the experience rewarding.

My Take:

Embrace the challenges that come with pursuing your passions. Difficulties and obstacles are part of the journey and learning to navigate them with grace will make the rewards even sweeter.

4. Stay Humble and Keep Learning

RaZZ emphasised the importance of humility in his career. Even as an experienced pilot, he continually learns from others, including instructors and fellow pilots. Staying open to feedback and criticism is vital to improving performance.

My Take:

No matter how skilled you become, there's always room for growth. Keep a mindset of continuous learning and be willing to accept feedback from others to continually refine your skills.

5. Appreciate the Moment

A key motto for the F-22 Demonstration Team is "How lucky are we?" This phrase serves as a reminder to appreciate the incredible opportunity they have to do what they love, even in the face of challenges and a demanding schedule.

My Take:

Gratitude can shift your mindset and help you find joy in your work. No matter how challenging your day may be, take a moment to appreciate the opportunities you've been given.

APPLYING THE LESSONS TO LIFE

Samuel Larson's insights offer valuable lessons for anyone looking to improve their performance and mindset, regardless of their field. Here are some ways to apply his teachings:

- **Visualise your success**: Before any major task or event, take a few moments to mentally walk through the steps. Visualisation helps build confidence and clarity.

- **Focus on teamwork**: Whether in business, sports, or any collaborative endeavour, ensure you're working with a supportive team that shares the same goals and values.

- **Accept challenges**: Don't shy away from the hard work. Embrace the challenges you face, knowing that they will make you stronger in the long run.

- **Stay humble**: Always be open to learning, even if you're at the top of your field. Humility and a growth mindset are key to long-term success.

- **Practice gratitude**: Regularly remind yourself of how fortunate you are to be doing what you love and let that gratitude fuel your passion and perseverance.

APPLY THE LESSONS: REFLECTION QUESTIONS

1. How can you incorporate visualisation techniques into your daily routine to improve performance in high-pressure situations?

2. In what ways can you foster stronger teamwork in your personal or professional life?

3. What challenges are you currently facing that you could embrace instead of avoiding?

4. How can you adopt a mindset of continuous learning, even if you consider yourself an expert in your field?

5. What are you grateful for in your current work or life situation and how can that sense of gratitude help you stay motivated?

Website, links, projects & contact available on pages 205-214

LOUIS SKUPIEN

CHAPTER 18: GREG WOOLDRIDGE
THE BLUEPRINT FOR ELITE TEAMWORK AND LEADERSHIP

INTRODUCTION

Greg "Boss" Wooldridge, the only person to have served three separate tours as the commanding officer of the U.S. Navy's Blue Angels, offers unparalleled insight into leadership and precision in high-performance environments. This chapter dives into Greg's journey from an aspiring pilot to leading the world's most famous aerobatic team. His lessons on resilience, teamwork and trust are as applicable to life on the ground as they are to the skies, demonstrating how discipline, character and compassion drive elite performance in any field.

EPISODE SUMMARY

Greg Wooldridge's aviation career was far from typical. Raised in the Midwest of the U.S., Greg initially didn't plan on becoming a pilot, let alone the leader of the Blue Angels. His journey started with building model airplanes and a fascination with flight but took off in earnest after joining the Navy. Greg's career led him through various squadrons, mastering air combat and eventually taking on leadership roles. His time in command was defined by the trust and camaraderie built within the Blue Angels—an environment where precision was paramount and mistakes could mean life or death. Greg's leadership style fostered an atmosphere where team members supported one another and always strived for perfection. Despite the pressure of performing in front of millions, Greg's leadership philosophy emphasises the importance of humility, gratitude and constant self-improvement.

FIVE KEY LESSONS

1. Leadership Through Gratitude

The culture of the Blue Angels is built on a foundation of trust and gratitude. Greg speaks about the importance of appreciating everyone around you, no matter their role. This creates an atmosphere where every team member feels valued and motivated to give their best.

My Take:

In any organisation, gratitude and respect lay the groundwork for high performance. By showing appreciation for everyone's contributions, you can foster a culture where people are more likely to take ownership and strive for excellence.

2. Trust as the Bedrock of Teamwork

Operating just 18 inches apart at 400 mph requires a level of trust that most of us will never experience. For Greg, building that trust among the Blue Angels was crucial to their success, not just in the air but in their daily lives.

My Take:

Trust is essential in any high-performance team. Whether in business or personal relationships, the ability to rely on others and to be reliable yourself is a cornerstone of success.

3. The Power of Debriefing

Greg emphasises the importance of debriefing after every flight. This process is not about blame but about learning from mistakes and continuously improving. The Blue Angels created a safe space for open communication, which led to constant refinement of their craft.

My Take:

Whether it's after a project or a personal challenge, reflecting on what went well and what didn't is key to growth. Implementing regular debriefs can ensure that you and your team are always learning and improving.

4. Character Over Skill

Surprisingly, the Blue Angels didn't select their team members based solely on flying skill. They were more concerned with personality and character, knowing that someone with the right attitude could learn the technical aspects of the job.

My Take:

Skills can be taught, but character is ingrained. In any field, hiring or collaborating with people who possess integrity, humility and a strong work ethic is far more valuable than technical ability alone.

5. Pursuing Excellence in Every Aspect

For Greg, the Blue Angels were never about the individual—it was about the team achieving something greater than themselves. Every member contributed to the success of the team and their performances were designed to inspire excellence in everyone who watched.

My Take:

Striving for excellence doesn't have to be limited to one area of life. Whether it's in your career, personal development, or relationships, aiming to be the best version of yourself will elevate those around you as well.

APPLYING THE LESSONS TO LIFE

Greg's insights into leadership and precision offer valuable lessons for anyone striving to achieve greatness. His philosophy of trust, gratitude and self-improvement can be applied to any area of life. Here's how you can incorporate these lessons:

- **Build trust:** Cultivate strong relationships based on trust and mutual respect.
- **Debrief regularly:** After completing any major task, reflect on the experience to identify areas for improvement.

- **Foster gratitude:** Show appreciation for those around you and create an environment where everyone feels valued.

- **Prioritise character:** Whether leading a team or building a network, focus on surrounding yourself with individuals who demonstrate integrity and humility.

- **Pursue excellence:** Strive to be your best in every aspect of life, knowing that this will inspire those around you to do the same.

APPLY THE LESSONS: REFLECTION QUESTIONS

1. How can you build trust with your team or those around you?

2. In what areas of your life can you implement regular debriefs to ensure continuous improvement?

3. How can you foster an environment of gratitude in your personal or professional life?

4. What steps can you take to prioritise character in your relationships and decisions?

5. What does excellence look like in your current role and how can you pursue it?

Website, links, projects & contact available on pages 205-214

CHAPTER 19: KRIS "TANTO" PARONTO
SURVIVING EVERYTHING THEY COULD THROW AT HIM

INTRODUCTION

Kris "Tanto" Paronto is best known for his role as a security contractor with the CIA, particularly during the 2012 attack on the U.S. diplomatic compound in Benghazi, Libya. His incredible journey, including his military background as an Army Ranger, contracting career and battle for survival in Benghazi, was portrayed in the book and film *13 Hours: The Secret Soldiers of Benghazi*. Kris has also authored books and launched his own training company, Battleline Tactical. In this chapter, we dive into his experiences, the mental fortitude needed for such high-stakes situations and the lessons that can be applied to everyday life.

EPISODE SUMMARY

Kris grew up in small-town America, not initially planning to enter the military. It wasn't until later in college, after seeing a recruiter and a captivating Army Ranger video, that he decided to enlist. His early military career, however, was not smooth.

Kris got into trouble and was discharged but later re-enlisted, determined to prove himself. He went through the gruelling process of becoming a Ranger and eventually found himself transitioning into contracting work for private companies like Blackwater and, later, the CIA.

The attack on Benghazi, which was immortalised in the movie *13 Hours*, thrust Kris into a situation where he and his teammates had to defend the U.S. compound after it was overrun by militants. Despite the lack of support and facing insurmountable odds, Kris and his team managed to save numerous lives, though they tragically lost some of their own.

Kris shares insights into how his training, mental preparation and team dynamics played crucial roles in their ability to survive and fight back. He also emphasises how these experiences shaped his outlook on adversity, resilience and the importance of never giving up.

FIVE KEY LESSONS

1. Adversity Builds Resilience

Kris's journey has been filled with ups and downs, from being kicked out of the military to facing life-threatening situations as a contractor. These moments of adversity only served to build his resilience. He emphasises that adversity should not be feared but embraced as an opportunity for growth and learning.

My Take:

Adversity can be one of life's greatest teachers. By facing challenges head-on and persevering, you develop the strength to overcome future obstacles.

2. Control Your Attitude

One of Kris's key takeaways from his experiences is the importance of controlling your attitude in any situation. While you may not always have control over external circumstances, you can always control how you react to them. This mindset allowed Kris to stay focused and calm, even in the most chaotic environments.

My Take:

Your attitude shapes your reality. By maintaining a positive and determined outlook, you can navigate through even the toughest challenges with grace and resilience.

3. Training and Preparation Are Critical

Kris credits much of his survival in Benghazi to the years of training and preparation he had undergone as a Ranger and contractor. Training for worst-case scenarios ensures that, when faced with real danger, you can act without hesitation and make decisions that can save lives.

My Take:

Preparation is key to success in any field. Whether in business, fitness, or personal challenges, consistently honing your skills prepares you to excel when it truly matters.

4. Teamwork and Trust

In Benghazi, Kris and his teammates had to rely on each other in life-or-death situations. The trust and camaraderie built over years of working together were crucial in their ability to operate as a cohesive unit under extreme pressure.

My Take:

The strength of any team lies in the trust and cooperation between its members. Whether in a professional or personal setting, cultivating strong relationships and mutual respect is essential for success.

5. Never Give Up

Despite being outnumbered and outgunned, Kris and his team never gave up. They fought until they had no other option and, in the process, saved many lives. Kris explains that the ability to keep pushing forward, no matter the odds, is what defines true resilience.

My Take:

Persistence is key to overcoming any challenge. No matter how difficult things may seem, keep pushing forward and never lose hope.

APPLYING THE LESSONS TO LIFE

Kris Paronto's story is a testament to the power of resilience, mental fortitude and the importance of never giving up, no matter the odds. Here are some ways to apply his lessons to your life:

- Embrace adversity: See challenges as opportunities for growth and development rather than obstacles.

- Control your attitude: Focus on what you can control—your attitude and response to situations.

- Prepare yourself: Invest time in training and improving your skills so you can act decisively when needed.

- Build strong teams: Trust and collaboration are vital in both personal and professional settings.

- Never give up: No matter the odds, maintain persistence and keep moving forward.

APPLY THE LESSONS: REFLECTION QUESTIONS

- How do you typically respond to adversity? Can you think of ways to embrace challenges rather than avoid them?

- What steps can you take to maintain a positive attitude when faced with difficult situations?

- Are you prepared for the challenges you might face in your personal or professional life? How can you improve your readiness?

- How can you foster stronger trust and collaboration within your team?

- When was the last time you felt like giving up and how did you push through it? How can you apply that same resilience to future challenges?

Website, links, projects & contact available on pages 205-214

CHAPTER 20: TREY RAWLS
THE ART OF LEADERSHIP AND RISK-TAKING

INTRODUCTION

Major General Trey Rawls, a retired two-star officer of the United States Air Force, brings decades of wisdom from an extraordinary career. From flying the A-10 Warthog and F-15 Eagle to overseeing cutting-edge advancements in the F-35 program, Trey's journey encapsulates a life dedicated to excellence, leadership and pushing boundaries. In this chapter, we dive into his career highlights, philosophies on leadership and his nuanced understanding of risk. His story not only offers a glimpse into the intricate world of military aviation and operational testing but also serves as a guide for anyone aspiring to lead and excel in their chosen field.

EPISODE SUMMARY

Major General Trey Rawls didn't always know he wanted to be a fighter pilot. Born and raised in Kentucky, he grew up in a state without an Air Force base and with limited exposure to aviation. A chance encounter with an inspiring Air Force colonel shifted his trajectory, leading Trey to a scholarship through the ROTC program at the University of Kentucky, where he studied electrical engineering. That meeting planted the seed for a remarkable career spanning over three decades.

Trey began his journey flying the A-10 Warthog in combat missions, later transitioning to the F-15 Eagle, a platform he describes as his "first love." He attended the Air Force Test Pilot School, flew over 30 different aircraft and commanded at multiple levels, culminating in his role as the Commander of the Air Force Operational Test and Evaluation Center (AFOTEC). There, he evaluated programs worth over $1 trillion, ensuring their combat readiness and operational effectiveness.

Throughout his career, Trey emphasised the importance of relationships, decisive leadership and calculated risk-taking. From his time working with NATO to developing multi-domain operational capabilities, Trey's ability to adapt and innovate has been a hallmark of his success. His reflections offer timeless lessons on leadership, perseverance and pursuing excellence.

FIVE KEY LESSONS

1. Relationships Are Everything

Trey believes that relationships form the cornerstone of effective leadership. In every stage of his career, building trust and fostering strong connections with others proved essential to achieving success.

My Take:

Whether in the military, business, or personal life, the relationships you nurture will define your trajectory. People will remember how you made them feel and the environment you created more than any specific task or project. Prioritise authenticity and empathy to build lasting connections.

2. Embrace the Power of Decisiveness

As Trey explains, great leaders make decisions with clarity and conviction. While collaboration is critical, decision-making ultimately rests on the shoulders of the leader. Hesitation can derail progress.

My Take:

Decisiveness is a hallmark of leadership. In moments of uncertainty, assess the facts, consult your team and act confidently. Even if the outcome isn't perfect, taking decisive action shows strength and inspires trust.

3. Learn from Failure and Debrief Regularly

One of Trey's defining leadership practices is the willingness to admit mistakes. In the fighter pilot community, debriefing after every mission is a cornerstone of improvement, where errors are acknowledged and used as a foundation for growth.

My Take:

Debriefing is essential for growth, whether in aviation, business, or personal pursuits. Cultivate a mindset that views mistakes as opportunities to learn rather than setbacks to fear. This approach fosters resilience and continual progress.

4. Take Calculated Risks

Trey advocates for taking thoughtful risks, differentiating between reckless gambling and calculated decisions. Risk-taking is essential for innovation and progress, but it must be approached with preparation and awareness.

My Take:

Avoid playing it safe out of fear, but don't gamble on uninformed decisions. Evaluate the potential rewards, weigh the consequences and mitigate risks wherever possible. Remember: growth lies on the other side of discomfort.

5. Focus on Excellence Over Mediocrity

Rather than striving to be average at many things, Trey emphasises honing your strengths to achieve greatness. Identify what you're naturally good at and dedicate yourself to becoming world-class in those areas.

My Take:

True success comes from excelling in your unique strengths. Shift your focus from improving weaknesses to mastering your passions and talents. Surround yourself with others who complement your abilities to create a well-rounded team.

APPLYING THE LESSONS TO LIFE

Trey Rawls 'story is not just one of personal achievement; it's a blueprint for aspiring leaders and innovators. Here's how you can incorporate his lessons into your own journey:

- **Build strong relationships:** Seek out mentors, surround yourself with supportive peers and invest in the people around you. Relationships are the foundation of success.

- **Decide with confidence:** Trust your judgment and act decisively when the moment calls for it. Indecision can stall opportunities.

- **Debrief your life:** Reflect on successes and failures alike. Use feedback to refine your approach and grow continuously.

- **Take risks wisely:** Stretch beyond your comfort zone, but always evaluate the potential outcomes. Growth requires risk, but recklessness wastes opportunities.

- **Master your strengths:** Focus on what you excel at and double down on developing those skills to their fullest potential.

APPLY THE LESSONS: REFLECTION QUESTIONS

1. How can you strengthen relationships in your personal and professional life to create a foundation for success?

2. When faced with a decision, how can you approach it with greater decisiveness and confidence?

3. How often do you reflect on your actions and how can a regular debrief process enhance your growth?

4. What calculated risks can you take to push yourself closer to your goals?

5. What are your core strengths and how can you develop them into world-class skills?

CHAPTER 21: EDDIE PENNEY
THE TIP OF THE SPEAR IN ANTI-TERRORISM

INTRODUCTION

Eddie Penney, a retired Navy SEAL and former member of SEAL Team Six, has taken his military experience and used it to build a successful career in business and personal development. As the founder of Contingent Group and the *Unafraid* brand, Eddie applies the lessons he learned from combat and elite training to help others overcome fear and take control of their lives. This chapter explores Eddie's journey from the military to entrepreneurship, his struggles with transition and the mindset that has helped him and others become unafraid.

EPISODE SUMMARY

Eddie Penney grew up with a love for the outdoors and a fascination with military action, spurred by action movies and real-life military heroes. His military career began in the U.S. Marine Corps before transitioning to the Navy SEALs. Eddie spent six years with the elite SEAL Team Six, where he participated in seven combat deployments across Iraq, Afghanistan and Africa. Eddie recalls the pride and purpose he found in his role, focusing not on the fame of individual missions, but on the mission of eliminating evil from the world.

After retiring from the military, Eddie faced significant challenges adjusting to civilian life. The loss of structure and support led him to struggle with alcohol and pill use. However, Eddie found strength in his faith and his role as a father, using those as catalysts to build a new chapter in his life. Eddie's *Unafraid* brand is more than a name; it's a reflection of his belief that fear should never hold people back from achieving their potential. Through his business ventures and personal development platforms, Eddie now helps others confront their fears and push through life's challenges.

FIVE KEY LESSONS

1. Overcoming Fear is a Choice

Fear is a universal experience, but Eddie emphasises that everyone has a choice when they encounter it. He explains that fear doesn't have to dictate your actions; it's a matter of deciding to push through rather than letting it consume you.

My Take:

Fear is natural, but letting it stop you from achieving your goals isn't. The power lies in deciding to push through those feelings and continue toward your aspirations, no matter how daunting the obstacles may seem.

2. Take an Honest Inventory of Your Life

Eddie suggests taking an inventory of toxic elements in your life—whether it's people, places, habits, or even thoughts.

Writing down what needs to change can help you make a plan to remove those toxic influences and focus on healthier ones.

My Take:

Taking stock of your life and identifying what's holding you back is an important first step. Once you're clear about the toxic elements, you can take targeted actions to eliminate them and make room for growth.

3. Success in Business and Life Requires a 'Make It Happen' Mentality

Eddie talks about how, in combat, failure to act often means the difference between life and death. This sense of urgency and responsibility translated directly into his business ventures. In both business and life, he adopts a "make it happen" mindset—whatever the challenge, there's always a way to get it done.

My Take:

Having a mindset that anything is possible can propel you forward in life and business. By believing that challenges can be overcome and that success is attainable, you position yourself to achieve more than you thought possible.

4. Continuous Self-Improvement is Key

Despite his accomplishments, Eddie believes in the importance of constant self-improvement. He admits that while he may have certain areas of life mastered, he still has personal weaknesses to work on, including patience and managing anger.

My Take:

We're all works in progress and self-improvement should be a continuous journey. No matter how successful you become, there's always room to grow, evolve and refine yourself both personally and professionally.

5. Surround Yourself with Positive Influences

Eddie stresses the importance of cutting out toxic people and environments, while focusing on building relationships with those who lift you up and support your goals. Whether in business, personal life, or mental well-being, the company you keep has a massive impact on your success.

My Take:

The people around you have a huge influence on your mindset and behaviour. Surrounding yourself with supportive, positive people will elevate your life, while cutting out toxic influences allows you to focus on what really matters.

APPLYING THE LESSONS TO LIFE

Eddie Penney's story and philosophy are rooted in the principles of pushing past fear, taking responsibility for your life and constantly striving to improve. Here are some ways to apply his teachings to your own life:

- Write down a list of toxic elements in your life, from people to habits and take steps to eliminate them.
- Commit to a "make it happen" mindset in your personal and professional life, refusing to let obstacles stop you.

- Be honest with yourself about your weaknesses and focus on continuous self-improvement.

- Surround yourself with positive influences that push you toward your goals rather than holding you back.

- Don't let fear dictate your actions—push through it and achieve what you once thought impossible.

APPLY THE LESSONS: REFLECTION QUESTIONS

- What fears are currently holding you back and how can you start pushing through them to reach your goals?

- What toxic elements in your life need to be removed and how can you start taking steps to eliminate them today?

- In what areas of your life could adopting a "make it happen" mindset propel you forward?

- What personal weaknesses are you working on and how can you create a plan for self-improvement?

- Are the people in your life supporting your growth and success, or do they hold you back? How can you adjust your circle of influence to benefit your journey?

Website, links, projects & contact available on pages 205-214

LOUIS SKUPIEN

CHAPTER 22: LANCE POWER
DEFENDING THE FREE WORLD FROM CYBER THREATS

INTRODUCTION

Lance Power, Command Chief of the 67th Cyberspace Wing in the United States Air Force, brings a wealth of experience and knowledge to the realm of cyberspace operations. As the leader of over 3,000 Airmen in America's premier cyber wing, Lance provides unique insights into the rapidly evolving digital battlefield. In this chapter, we delve into his career, his perspectives on leadership and the critical role his team plays in ensuring the security and readiness of the United States Air Force.

EPISODE SUMMARY

Lance Power's journey began in Indiana, where he joined the United States Air Force straight out of high school, initially planning to serve for just four years. Over 27 years later, he has built a distinguished career in the Air Force, witnessing and contributing to pivotal moments in history, including September

11, 2001, when he played a crucial role in facilitating communications for Air Force One.

Transitioning from a radio operator to a leader in the cyber domain, Lance experienced the growing importance of cyberspace as a war-fighting domain. Now at the helm of the 67th Cyberspace Wing, Lance oversees operations critical to the defence of America's "digital skies." His role includes ensuring that his team is prepared to defend against adversarial threats, protect critical infrastructure and work with allies to strengthen global cyber defences.

Throughout his career, Lance has prioritised teamwork, leadership and adaptability. From deploying to Afghanistan to teaching leadership in Germany, his experiences shaped his approach to guiding one of the Air Force's most innovative units. His personal journey, including the challenges and triumphs of becoming a father to twins, further exemplifies his resilience and dedication.

Lance Power's insights into the cyber domain highlight the increasing importance of adaptability, collaboration and a relentless pursuit of excellence in both military and civilian contexts.

FIVE KEY LESSONS

1. The Importance of Cybersecurity

Lance emphasises that the cyber domain is critical to national security, with potential threats evolving daily. His team's mission includes protecting the Air Force's digital infrastructure and collaborating with allies to counteract cyber threats.

My Take:

Cybersecurity is no longer optional—it is essential. Whether in government, business, or personal life, maintaining vigilance against cyber threats protects not only data but also critical systems that underpin modern society. Prioritising cybersecurity measures is a necessity in today's interconnected world.

2. Leadership Through Adaptability

Lance's career path underscores the importance of adaptability. From working as a radio operator to leading a cyber wing, his ability to pivot and embrace new roles has been instrumental in his success.

My Take:

In a rapidly changing world, adaptability is key to staying relevant. Embracing new challenges, learning continuously and stepping outside of comfort zones are critical for growth, whether in a career or personal endeavours.

3. The Value of Teamwork

The 67th Cyberspace Wing operates as a cohesive unit, with every Airman playing a vital role in mission success. Lance highlights the significance of fostering trust and collaboration within the team to achieve collective goals.

My Take:

No mission is accomplished alone. Building strong teams with mutual respect and clear communication is fundamental to success in any environment. Invest in your team and watch the outcomes exceed expectations.

4. Staying Ahead of Threats

Cyber threats evolve at an alarming pace, requiring constant innovation and vigilance. Lance's team continuously trains to anticipate and counteract adversarial actions in cyberspace.

My Take:

Proactivity beats reactivity. Whether in cyber defence or personal development, staying ahead of challenges requires a mindset focused on continuous improvement and staying informed.

5. Finding Purpose in Service

For Lance, his career has been defined by a sense of purpose and dedication to serving something greater than himself. This perspective has been a cornerstone of his leadership and motivation.

My Take:

Aligning your efforts with a greater purpose can transform work into a fulfilling journey. Find what drives you and let it guide your decisions and actions to create a meaningful impact.

APPLYING THE LESSONS TO LIFE

Lance Power's insights extend far beyond the cyber battlefield, offering valuable lessons for individuals from all walks of life. Here are practical ways to incorporate these lessons:

- **Prioritise cybersecurity:** Regularly update your devices, use strong passwords and remain vigilant about phishing scams.

- **Be adaptable:** Embrace change and seek opportunities to grow, even if it means stepping outside your comfort zone.

- **Foster teamwork:** Build trust and collaboration in your personal and professional relationships.

- **Stay informed:** Keep learning and stay ahead of trends in your industry or field.

- **Find purpose:** Reflect on what drives you and strive to align your work and personal goals with that purpose.

APPLY THE LESSONS: REFLECTION QUESTIONS

1. What steps can you take to improve your cybersecurity practices?

2. How do you adapt to change in your current environment?

3. Are you fostering a culture of trust and teamwork in your relationships or workplace?

4. How can you stay proactive in anticipating challenges in your field?

5. What purpose drives you and how can you align your actions with it?

Website, links, projects & contact available on pages 205-214

CHAPTER 23: MATTHEW "WHIZ" BUCKLEY
EXCELLING IN TOP GUN & BUSINESS

INTRODUCTION

Matthew "Whiz" Buckley, a retired Navy F/A-18 Hornet fighter pilot and graduate of the prestigious Top Gun program, brings his high-octane leadership lessons from the cockpit to the corporate world. After a successful military career, Whiz transitioned into the business sector, where he founded several companies, including Top Gun Options, a highly successful trading firm. In this chapter, we explore Whiz's journey from flying combat missions to building multimillion-dollar businesses and how the principles of military training shaped his approach to entrepreneurship and leadership.

EPISODE SUMMARY

Whiz Buckley grew up in a tight-knit Irish Catholic family in South Jersey, where he learned the values of service and duty from an early age. Inspired by his friend's father, a fighter pilot in the New Jersey Air National Guard, Whiz dreamed of flying jets off aircraft carriers. He pursued that dream, entering Navy flight school and eventually flying the F/A-18 Hornet, one of the Navy's most elite fighter jets.

Whiz graduated from Top Gun's adversary course, where he learned to be a "bad guy," studying enemy tactics to prepare the Navy's best pilots for combat. His career included combat missions over Iraq and later transitioning to a role as a reservist, flying fighter jets part-time while simultaneously building a career in finance.

On the morning of September 11, 2001, Whiz's life took a dramatic turn. After being furloughed from his airline job due to the tragic events of 9/11, he fully immersed himself in the world of trading, applying the precision, discipline and strategy from his military background to the financial markets. He eventually founded Top Gun Options, a firm that teaches retail investors how to trade options with the same intensity and focus as a fighter pilot on a mission.

FIVE KEY LESSONS

1. The Power of a Clear Mission Objective

Whiz emphasises that success starts with having a crystal-clear mission objective. In the military, there is no ambiguity about what needs to be accomplished. This same principle applies to business—everyone must be on the same page, understanding the exact goal and the metrics for success. Without clarity, teams become disjointed and ineffective.

My Take:

Clarity is essential for success. Whether in business, personal life, or any other endeavour, define your mission clearly, so every team member is aligned and working toward the same goal.

2. Single Point of Accountability

In the Navy, there is always a single person responsible for the success or failure of a mission. This concept of accountability is often missing in the business world, where multiple people share responsibilities without clear ownership. Whiz introduced the concept of the "Single Point of Accountability" to his businesses, ensuring that one person always held 51% of the responsibility for any task.

My Take:

Clear ownership leads to better execution. Assign responsibility clearly to ensure that someone is accountable for both success and failure.

3. Debriefing with Brutal Honesty

One of the most powerful tools Whiz carried from the military into his business ventures is the practice of debriefing. After every mission, military teams review what worked and what didn't, without pulling punches. This brutal honesty is critical for growth and improvement, yet it's often lacking in the corporate world, where people shy away from hard truths.

My Take:

Honest debriefs are key to improvement. In any project or endeavour, take time to reflect on what went wrong and how you can do better next time.

4. Contingency Planning

In aviation, pilots are trained to always prepare for the worst-case scenario. Contingency planning isn't something that happens when things go wrong; it's done beforehand. Whiz stressed the importance of anticipating challenges and having backup plans ready to execute in both the military and the business world.

My Take:

Prepare for the unexpected. Having a plan in place for worst-case scenarios allows you to react calmly and efficiently when things don't go as expected.

5. Applying Military Discipline to Business

Whiz believes that the discipline and structure instilled through military training are key to success in business. The methodologies, from setting clear objectives to rigorous planning and execution, are directly transferable from the battlefield to the boardroom.

My Take:

Discipline breeds success. By applying the structured, disciplined approach of military operations to business, you can achieve more consistent and reliable results.

APPLYING THE LESSONS TO LIFE

Matthew "Whiz" Buckley's journey provides a blueprint for turning military precision into business success. Here's how you can apply his principles to your own life:

- **Define your mission:** Whether personal or professional, ensure your goals are crystal clear and measurable.

- **Assign accountability:** Make sure someone is in charge, so there's a clear line of responsibility.

- **Debrief regularly:** Take time to reflect on what worked and what didn't. Brutal honesty will help you grow faster.

- **Plan for contingencies:** Always have a backup plan ready to go in case things don't go as expected.

- **Use military discipline:** Structure, routine and planning are key elements for success in any area of life.

APPLY THE LESSONS: REFLECTION QUESTIONS

- Do you have a clear mission for your current projects? What steps can you take to clarify your objectives?

- Who holds accountability in your team or business? How can you ensure clearer ownership of tasks?

- When was the last time you debriefed after a project or task? What can you learn from that experience to improve?

- Are you prepared for the unexpected? What contingency plans can you create for potential challenges in your current endeavours?

- How can you introduce more discipline and structure into your daily routine?

Website, links, projects & contact available on pages 205-214

CHAPTER 24: HELEN ISAAC
OVERCOMING ADVERSITY AND BUILDING A FITNESS LEGACY

INTRODUCTION

Helen Isaac, a personal trainer with a unique journey, has transformed her life and the lives of her clients through fitness. A former corporate professional in the fashion and beauty industries, Helen took charge of her health and overcame obesity and depression to create a new path for herself. Now a sought-after personal trainer and recent winner of the prestigious Muddy Stilettos award for Best PT in Somerset, Dorset and Bristol, Helen's story serves as a powerful testament to the life-changing benefits of fitness. In this chapter, we explore Helen's journey, her approach to personal training and the lessons we can all learn from her inspiring story.

EPISODE SUMMARY

Helen's path to fitness began after a family holiday, where she struggled to keep up with her daughter during a hike. Overweight, depressed and in poor health, Helen had a powerful realisation that she needed to make a change. This experience was a turning point and upon returning from the holiday, she took her first steps toward a healthier lifestyle.

Helen's journey was not easy. After years of fad diets, she joined a gym, learned about proper nutrition and gradually found a passion for exercise. Through her own transformation, she was inspired to help others. During lockdown, she began leading online workout classes for colleagues, which sparked her interest in personal training. Balancing a full-time job, motherhood and training, Helen earned her qualifications and launched her own business.

Her client-centric approach, focusing on building meaningful relationships and providing ongoing support, has led to her recognition as one of the top personal trainers in the region. Helen's unique perspective, as someone still on her own fitness journey, allows her to deeply empathise with her clients, many of whom are at the beginning of their own paths to better health.

FIVE KEY LESSONS

1. Transforming Through Adversity

Helen's fitness journey began in a place of adversity, battling obesity and depression. Her story is a reminder that even in our lowest moments, change is possible. She took control of her life, prioritising health and well-being, which led to profound physical and mental transformations.

My Take:

Adversity can often be the catalyst for personal growth. When you feel like you're at your lowest, that's the time to make a change. Embrace those moments as opportunities to redefine your life.

2. The Power of Community

Helen emphasises the importance of a supportive community in the gym environment. She believes that gyms should be places where people feel motivated and supported rather than intimidated. This sense of community plays a crucial role in maintaining consistency and achieving long-term success.

My Take:

Surrounding yourself with a positive, supportive community is key to staying motivated in any endeavour. Whether it's in the gym or in life, having people who believe in you makes all the difference.

3. Quality Over Quantity in Personal Training

Helen's business model focuses on developing deep, lasting relationships with her clients. She believes in prioritising quality over quantity, taking the time to truly invest in each client's journey. This approach not only leads to better results but also creates a loyal client base.

My Take:

In any business, focusing on quality over quantity allows you to build trust and deliver meaningful results. By truly investing in others, you create lasting impact and foster loyalty.

4. Exercise is More Than Physical

For Helen, fitness isn't just about physical appearance—it's about mental well-being and creating a lifestyle that fosters happiness. Her personal experience with exercise as a means of overcoming depression has shaped her approach to personal training, where she encourages clients to see exercise as a way to improve overall well-being.

My Take:

Exercise should be viewed as a tool for enhancing all aspects of life, not just physical fitness. It can help reduce stress, improve mood and provide a sense of accomplishment and balance.

5. Balancing Life and Fitness

Helen balances motherhood, business and her own health challenges with leukaemia, all while running a successful personal training business. Her ability to juggle these responsibilities serves as an inspiration to others who may feel overwhelmed by the demands of life.

My Take:

Balance is key to sustaining success. While life can throw many challenges your way, prioritising health and well-being is essential for navigating those challenges with grace and strength.

APPLYING THE LESSONS TO LIFE

Helen Isaac's journey highlights the power of persistence, community and balance in creating a fulfilling life through fitness. Her story shows that anyone, regardless of where they start, can achieve their goals with the right mindset and support. Here's how you can apply her lessons:

- Embrace adversity: Use challenging moments as a springboard for growth and change.

- Build a support system: Surround yourself with people who encourage and uplift you, whether in the gym or in life.

- Focus on relationships: Whether in business or personal life, quality relationships are the key to success and fulfilment.

- See fitness as holistic: Exercise is not just about looking good; it's about feeling good mentally and emotionally too.

- Strive for balance: No matter how busy life gets, make time for the things that matter, including your health and well-being.

APPLY THE LESSONS: REFLECTION QUESTIONS

- What challenges in your life can you use as a catalyst for positive change?

- How can you build a stronger sense of community in your life, whether in fitness or other areas?

- Are you prioritising quality over quantity in your relationships or work? How can you improve in this area?

- How do you view exercise? Is it just about physical fitness, or can you shift your perspective to see its broader benefits?

- How can you better balance your personal and professional life to prioritise your health and well-being?

Website, links, projects & contact available on pages 205-214

CHAPTER 25: JON "FIZZLE" FAY
LEADING WITH PRECISION AND TRUST IN THE BLUE ANGELS

INTRODUCTION

Jon "Fizzle" Fay, Executive Officer of the United States Navy's Blue Angels, shares a remarkable insight into the world of Naval Aviation and the iconic Blue Angels team. In this chapter, we explore Jon's journey, from his upbringing in Texas to his leadership role in one of the most prestigious demonstration teams in the world. His dedication to precision, trust and a culture of excellence drives home the importance of teamwork and the high standards expected of those who represent the United States Navy and Marine Corps.

EPISODE SUMMARY

Jon Fay's journey began in Fort Worth, Texas, where he developed an early fascination with aviation, fuelled by airshows and the F-16 fighter jets produced at the local General Dynamics plant. Raised in a family that valued character and discipline, Jon's path led him to the United States Naval Academy, where he committed to a life of service. While he initially aspired to be a pilot, his journey took an unexpected turn, leading him to a distinguished career as a Naval Flight Officer flying the S-3B Viking and P-3C Orion.

Today, Jon Fay serves as the Executive Officer of the Blue Angels, a position responsible for assisting the commanding officer and ensuring the smooth execution of policies and operations. The Blue Angels 'mission extends beyond flight demonstrations, aiming to inspire excellence and patriotism in every individual who witnesses their performances. Jon shares the demanding nature of flying at high speeds, close to the ground, in precise formations. He emphasises that the Blue Angels' success stems from unwavering trust, teamwork and relentless dedication to perfection. Despite the highly visible nature of their performances, it's the character and values behind the team that truly set them apart.

FIVE KEY LESSONS

1. The Importance of Trust and Teamwork

The Blue Angels operate in high-pressure environments where even the slightest error could have significant consequences. Trust and teamwork are the bedrock of their success. Each team member must rely on the others, knowing that precision flying depends on a collective effort, where every action counts.

My Take:

Trust and teamwork are essential not just in aviation but in any endeavour. The strongest teams are those where each individual knows their role and understands that their success depends on the success of the team. In business and life, fostering a deep sense of trust and collaboration can take your efforts to new heights.

2. Relentless Pursuit of Precision

In the Blue Angels, precision is a non-negotiable standard. Pilots practice their routines repeatedly, visualising each manoeuvre to ensure perfection. Their performance, down to the last detail, is designed to inspire and demonstrate what is possible when you commit fully to excellence.

My Take:

The pursuit of precision in our daily tasks can elevate outcomes from average to extraordinary. Whether it's in your work, personal goals, or relationships, aiming for precision means you are always striving for your best, leaving little room for error. It's not about perfection; it's about setting high standards and consistently meeting them.

3. The Value of Debriefing

After each flight demonstration, the Blue Angels debrief meticulously. They review every aspect of the performance, identify mistakes and discuss improvements. No flight is perfect, but the constant analysis and feedback loop ensure continuous improvement.

My Take:

Debriefing is an essential practice for any team or individual striving for growth. Whether after a project at work, a sports game, or a personal endeavour, reflecting on what went well and what didn't creates opportunities for learning and growth. It allows you to evolve and avoid repeating mistakes, ensuring you're always moving forward.

4. Character Drives Performance

While precision and teamwork are critical to the Blue Angels' success, Jon emphasises that character is what truly drives performance. The team's culture is built on integrity, discipline and an unwavering commitment to being the best version of themselves—both in the air and on the ground.

My Take:

Character is the foundation of sustained success. Skills and talent can take you far, but without a strong moral compass and dedication to personal integrity, long-term achievement is unlikely. By focusing on building your character—being honest, disciplined and driven—you create a solid base for excelling in any area of life.

5. Failure as a Learning Opportunity

Jon reflects on how his career didn't follow the exact path he envisioned and how setbacks, including not getting selected for the Blue Angels on his first try, were opportunities for growth. The Blue Angels have never flown a perfect flight, but their relentless pursuit of excellence means they learn from each failure and strive for improvement.

My Take:

Failure is not the end—it's a steppingstone toward success. The ability to learn from failure and move forward is what differentiates those who grow from those who stay stagnant. By reframing setbacks as lessons, you can continue to improve and ultimately reach your goals.

APPLYING THE LESSONS TO LIFE

Jon Fay's insights from his time with the Blue Angels offer a powerful blueprint for anyone looking to excel in life, whether personally or professionally. His emphasis on trust, teamwork, precision and character applies to a wide range of disciplines beyond aviation. Here are some practical ways to incorporate these lessons:

- **Foster teamwork:** Build a culture of trust and collaboration in your environment, whether it's at work, home, or in your community.

- **Pursue precision:** Commit to doing things to the best of your ability, paying attention to detail and striving for excellence in every task.

- **Debrief regularly:** After completing a major project or task, reflect on what worked and what could be improved. Make this a regular practice to ensure continual growth.

- **Build strong character:** Let integrity and discipline guide your decisions. Be consistent in your actions and hold yourself accountable to high standards.

- **Embrace failure:** See failure as an opportunity to learn. Don't shy away from mistakes—instead, analyse them and use the experience to improve.

APPLY THE LESSONS: REFLECTION QUESTIONS

- How can you build trust and foster teamwork in your current environment?

- In what areas of your life can you practice greater precision and attention to detail?

- Do you regularly reflect on your actions and performance? How can a debrief process benefit you or your team?

- How can you work on developing your character to become a better version of yourself?

- What recent failure or setback can you reframe as a learning experience and how can you use it to move forward?

Website, links, projects & contact available on pages 205-214

CHAPTER 26: CRAIG HARRISON
PRECISION DEFINED BY A SNIPER WORLD RECORD HOLDER

INTRODUCTION

Craig Harrison, a former British Army sniper, held the world record for the longest confirmed sniper kill at an incredible 2,475 meters. Serving 23 years in the military, 16 of which were spent as a front-line sniper, Craig completed 10 tours of duty. His journey from a young soldier with aspirations to become a farrier, to an elite sniper who saved lives on the battlefield, is a remarkable story of perseverance, adaptability and discipline. In this chapter, we delve into his military career, the challenges of being a sniper and the personal sacrifices he endured during and after his service.

EPISODE SUMMARY

Craig's journey into the British Army wasn't initially about becoming a sniper. Coming from a military family, Craig joined the Army with the goal of becoming a farrier. However, after encountering challenges due to his dyslexia, he had to adjust his career path. Despite these setbacks, Craig found his calling when he met a sniper during his time in Iraq. Inspired by the professionalism and independence that came with the role, Craig pursued the sniper path with determination.

After being the first in his regiment to become a sniper, Craig excelled in his career. His record-setting shot wasn't a planned feat of personal achievement; it was an act to save his comrades during a mission in Afghanistan. Using his elite marksmanship and tactical acumen, he successfully neutralised enemy combatants from over 2,475 meters away. However, the attention his record garnered came with severe personal consequences. After the media leaked his identity, Craig and his family faced death threats, forcing them into hiding for three years.

Craig's story is one of resilience in the face of adversity. His post-military life hasn't been easy as he deals with complex PTSD, but he's found solace through therapy, family support and helping others through his survival school, which provides a space for veterans struggling with mental health.

FIVE KEY LESSONS

1. Adaptability in the Face of Setbacks

Craig's original goal in the military was to become a farrier, but when that path didn't work out due to challenges related to his dyslexia, he had to find a new direction. Instead of giving up, he pivoted and pursued sniping, a role that ended up being perfectly suited to his strengths.

My Take:

Life rarely goes as planned, but adaptability is crucial for long-term success. Embrace change and when one path closes, look for new opportunities that might suit you even better.

2. Precision and Patience Are Key to Success

As a sniper, Craig learned the importance of patience and precision. His role required him to wait for the perfect moment to take a shot, often in high-stakes situations. This level of discipline and control over emotions ensured success on the battlefield.

My Take:

In life and business, rushing decisions can lead to mistakes. Learning to take a step back, evaluate the situation and make thoughtful, calculated moves can result in better outcomes.

3. Managing Stress with Breathing and Focus

In a high-stress environment, Craig relied on techniques like controlled breathing to calm himself down and stay focused. These techniques allowed him to make accurate decisions even in life-or-death scenarios.

My Take:

Learning how to manage stress through mindful breathing or other calming practices can make all the difference in your performance, whether in high-pressure business environments or personal situations.

4. Practice and Preparation Lead to Mastery

Craig emphasises that sniping is not about luck; it's about practice. Every element of a successful shot is rehearsed countless times before it ever happens in the field. Mastery comes from repetition and preparation.

My Take:

Whether in sports, business, or any field, continuous practice and preparation are the foundations of excellence. Success comes from refining your skills over time through consistent effort.

5. Resilience Through Support Systems

After his military career, Craig faced immense personal challenges, including PTSD and the fallout from media exposure. However, with the help of therapy and the support of his wife and family, he's been able to continue moving forward.

My Take:

Building and maintaining strong support systems is vital when facing difficult times. Whether through family, friends, or professional help, surrounding yourself with people who can offer support is key to overcoming life's challenges.

APPLYING THE LESSONS TO LIFE

Craig Harrison's journey offers powerful insights into discipline, resilience and adaptability. His approach to managing stress, practicing precision and relying on his support systems can be applied in everyday life, whether in personal development or professional growth. Here are some ways to implement his lessons:

- **Adapt when plans change:** When your original goals become unattainable, don't see it as failure. Instead, pivot and seek new opportunities.

- **Develop stress-management techniques:** Incorporating mindful breathing or other calming exercises can help you manage pressure in your career and personal life.

- **Commit to practice:** Mastery of any skill requires dedication and consistent practice. Make a habit of refining your abilities regularly.

- **Focus on precision:** Whether in decision-making or executing tasks, aim for accuracy and thoughtfulness over speed.

- **Build strong support networks:** Ensure you have a solid foundation of people who can support you through life's ups and downs.

APPLY THE LESSONS: REFLECTION QUESTIONS

- How can you adapt when life doesn't go as planned?

- What techniques can you incorporate into your daily routine to better manage stress and stay focused under pressure?

- Are there areas in your life where you can commit to more regular practice and preparation to improve your skills?

- How can you enhance precision and patience in your decision-making process?

- Who are the people in your life that offer support? How can you strengthen these relationships to ensure you have a reliable support system?

Website, links, projects & contact available on pages 205-214

CHAPTER 27: MILES DAISHER
JUMPING OFF EVERYTHING SO YOU DON'T HAVE TO!

INTRODUCTION

Miles Daisher is a pioneer in the world of extreme sports, particularly known for his base jumping and skydiving feats. With over 11,400 skydives and 7,000 base jumps, Miles holds an extraordinary position in the extreme sports community. His journey from a passion for thrill-seeking to working on major film productions like *Mission: Impossible – Dead Reckoning* showcases his dedication, courage and relentless drive. This chapter delves into Miles 'journey, his thoughts on fear, advice for those entering extreme sports and the preparation that goes into pulling off death-defying stunts safely and successfully.

EPISODE SUMMARY

Miles Daisher's path into extreme sports started with a dream of skydiving as a child. That dream turned into reality on September 6, 1995, when he completed his first skydive at the Yolo County Airport in Davis, California. Hooked from the very first jump, Miles quickly immersed himself in the sport, living at drop zones and progressing from packing parachutes to completing tandem jumps. His career skyrocketed as he delved into base jumping, honing his skills with friends like Shane McConkey and Mark Broderick, forming a close-knit team of jumpers.

Miles is not only passionate about jumping but also about safety and preparation. Every jump, whether it's off a bridge in his hometown of Twin Falls, Idaho, or from a remote cliff in Switzerland, involves meticulous planning, understanding weather conditions and ensuring physical and mental readiness. His ethos is built on a foundation of methodical preparation and a keen awareness of both the risks and the rewards.

In addition to his athletic achievements, Miles 'career has expanded into the entertainment world. He played a significant role in the recent *Mission: Impossible* film, working directly with Tom Cruise on one of the film's most dangerous stunts. His approach to high-risk activities is defined by careful planning, collaboration with a skilled team and the joy of pushing boundaries while always maintaining safety.

FIVE KEY LESSONS

1. Pursue Your Passion Relentlessly

Miles discovered his love for skydiving and base jumping early on and he followed that passion without hesitation. He left behind conventional paths to dedicate himself fully to the thrill of free-falling from planes, cliffs and bridges. His drive and determination have led him to become one of the top athletes in his field.

My Take:

Whatever your passion is, follow it with everything you've got. It may seem unconventional or risky to others, but if you pursue it relentlessly, you can achieve extraordinary things.

2. Safety First, Fun Always

While Miles may seem like a daredevil, he places a huge emphasis on safety and preparation. Every jump, no matter how routine, involves careful planning, situational awareness and weather assessment. His motto is clear: live in the moment, but always be fully prepared for the risks.

My Take:

In life, even when pursuing something thrilling or risky, preparation is key. Planning and understanding the potential risks will ensure not only your safety but also a better chance of success.

3. Face Your Fears Head-On

Miles often speaks about how fear never fully goes away, even after thousands of jumps. Instead, it becomes something you manage and use to stay alert and focused. For Miles, the excitement of overcoming fear and uncertainty is part of the rush.

My Take:

Fear is a natural part of any challenge. Instead of avoiding it, face it head-on and learn to use it to your advantage. It keeps you sharp and ensures you never get too comfortable.

4. Live in the Now

One of Miles 'core philosophies is living fully in the moment. Whether it's during a jump or in everyday life, he emphasises the importance of being present and focused. This mindset allows him to enjoy every experience fully and to react swiftly in high-stress situations.

My Take:

Being present is essential not only for extreme sports but for life in general. When you're fully engaged in the moment, you can make better decisions and enjoy the journey more thoroughly.

5. Always Be Ready to Learn and Adapt

Miles speaks about the importance of continuous learning, whether it's about new techniques, gear, or understanding different weather patterns. He also credits his success to his willingness to adapt to changing circumstances, ensuring he is always evolving as an athlete.

My Take:

Lifelong learning and adaptability are essential for growth. Stay curious and be willing to adjust your approach as new information comes to light, in both professional and personal pursuits.

APPLYING THE LESSONS TO LIFE

Miles Daisher's life offers powerful lessons for anyone looking to live more boldly and fully. Here are some ways you can apply his principles to your own life:

- Pursue what you love with full dedication, even if it seems unconventional or risky to others.

- Prioritise safety and preparation in everything you do, balancing excitement with responsibility.

- Face your fears and use them as fuel to keep you sharp and focused in high-pressure situations.

- Practice being present in every moment, whether in your work, relationships, or hobbies.

- Embrace continuous learning and adaptability to stay at the top of your game.

APPLY THE LESSONS: REFLECTION QUESTIONS

- What passion in your life are you holding back from pursuing fully?

- How can you better prepare for the challenges you face in life, whether personal or professional?

- In what ways can you embrace fear rather than let it hold you back?

- Are you living fully in the present, or are distractions preventing you from enjoying the moment?

- How can you ensure that you're always learning and growing, no matter how successful you become?

Website, links, projects & contact available on pages 205-214

CHAPTER 28: MICHAEL SARRAILLE
LEADERSHIP FROM A NAVY SEAL

INTRODUCTION

Michael Sarraille, a former Navy SEAL and Recon Marine, has led an impressive career that spans the battlefield and the boardroom. With over 20 years of military service, including 10 combat deployments, Michael has transitioned into the business world as an entrepreneur, speaker and leadership expert. He is the author of *The Talent War* and *The Everyday Warrior* and he leads initiatives such as Men's Journal's *Everyday Warrior*. His journey offers deep insights into resilience, leadership and high-performing teams, blending the intensity of Special Operations with practical business wisdom. In this chapter, we explore Michael's path from the SEAL Teams to his role as a leader in the private sector, focusing on the principles that guided his success.

EPISODE SUMMARY

Michael's route to becoming a Navy SEAL was unconventional. He began his military career in the Marine Corps as a Recon Marine and Scout Sniper before transitioning to the SEALs. Motivated by a desire to be part of the top Special Operations force, Michael endured the legendary SEAL training, driven by a combination of pride, camaraderie and a desire to be in the fight during the height of the War on Terror.

His SEAL career included deployments to Iraq, where he participated in major battles such as the Battle of Ramadi. Michael's leadership in combat was informed by a deep commitment to his team and he prioritised love and accountability as the core of his leadership philosophy.

After leaving the military, Michael transitioned into the business world, where he has founded several companies and now leads initiatives aimed at building leadership and mental resilience. He continues to apply the lessons he learned in the SEALs to his work with executives and high-performing teams, emphasising the importance of discipline, accountability and continuous learning.

FIVE KEY LESSONS

1. Leadership Through Love

Michael believes that the core of effective leadership is love—loving your team more than you hate the enemy. He emphasised that holding people accountable is the highest form of compassion because it shows you care about their growth and success. This principle guided him throughout his military career and continues to inform his approach to leadership in business.

My Take:

Leadership is about putting your people first and showing that you care about their success. When you lead with compassion and hold your team accountable, you create an environment where they can thrive and achieve great things.

2. Failure as a Mentor

In Michael's view, failure is not a reflection of your character but rather an essential learning tool. In the SEAL Teams, failure was used as a way to refine tactics, improve performance and build stronger leaders. He believes that accepting failure and learning from it is crucial for personal and professional growth.

My Take:

Failure should be embraced as part of the learning process. It provides valuable lessons that can help you improve and reach your goals. Don't fear failure; use it as a stepping stone to success.

3. Simplicity in Execution

One of the key lessons Michael learned in both combat and business is the importance of simplicity. Overcomplicating a plan can lead to confusion and failure. In Special Operations, simplicity is seen as the ultimate form of communication. Keeping things clear and focused is essential to success, whether on the battlefield or in the boardroom.

My Take:

Simplicity is powerful. Whether you're leading a team or working on a personal goal, stripping things down to their essential elements allows you to execute more effectively and stay focused on what matters most.

4. Continuous Training and Mentorship

Michael credits his success in both the military and business to the constant training and mentorship he received. Great leaders are forged, not born and they are made through consistent coaching, feedback and learning. This approach helped Michael develop the skills needed to lead elite teams and build successful businesses.

My Take:

Lifelong learning is critical to personal and professional development. Seek out mentors, embrace feedback and commit to continuous improvement in all areas of your life.

5. The Power of Self-Discipline

One of the main themes in Michael's philosophy is the importance of self-discipline. Leading yourself with accountability and consistency is the foundation for leading others. He stresses that you cannot lead others effectively until you first master leading yourself.

My Take:

Self-discipline is the cornerstone of success. By holding yourself accountable and staying committed to your goals, you create the foundation for achieving greatness in every area of your life.

APPLYING THE LESSONS TO LIFE

Michael Sarraille's approach to leadership and resilience is rooted in the principles he learned in the military, but they are universally applicable. Here's how you can apply his teachings to your own life:

- Lead with love: Whether in business or personal life, show care and compassion for the people around you by holding them accountable and supporting their growth.

- Embrace failure: Don't let setbacks discourage you. Instead, view them as valuable learning opportunities that will help you grow.

- Keep things simple: Focus on clear, actionable steps in any plan. Simplicity in execution leads to better results and less confusion.

- Seek continuous improvement: Always be open to learning and improving. Find mentors, seek feedback and push yourself to grow.

- Lead yourself first: Cultivate self-discipline and accountability in your own life before expecting to lead others effectively.

APPLY THE LESSONS: REFLECTION QUESTIONS

- How can you show more compassion and accountability in your leadership style?

- What recent failures can you reframe as learning opportunities and how will you use them to improve?

- Are there areas of your life where you are overcomplicating things? How can you simplify your approach to achieve better results?

- Who are the mentors in your life that can help you grow and how can you seek out more learning opportunities?

- How can you improve your self-discipline and accountability in your daily routine?

Website, links, projects & contact available on pages 205-214

CHAPTER 29: JOSHUA "CABO" GUNDERSON

LESSONS IN LEADERSHIP, INSPIRATION AND THE RAPTOR'S LEGACY

INTRODUCTION

Joshua "Cabo" Gunderson is a former F-15 Eagle and F-22 Raptor fighter pilot, whose career highlights include serving as Commander of the elite F-22 Demo Team. In this chapter, we delve into Cabo's inspiring journey, from his aviation aspirations as a young boy in Tampa, Florida, to his time leading one of the most advanced fighter aircraft in the world. Through his stories, he shares powerful insights about leadership, teamwork and the enduring power of inspiration.

Cabo's unique experiences provide valuable lessons, not just for those in aviation but for anyone striving to overcome challenges and achieve greatness. His commitment to empowering the next generation of dreamers highlights the impact of mentorship and the importance of building meaningful connections.

EPISODE SUMMARY

Growing up in Tampa, Florida, Cabo was fascinated by fighter jets from an early age. His passion for aviation was ignited at an airshow where he first saw the F-15 in action. Despite coming from a family without a military or aviation background, Cabo pursued his dream relentlessly. He graduated from the U.S. Air Force Academy, where he excelled in academics, leadership training and even taught in the glider program.

Cabo's career spanned both the F-15 Eagle and the F-22 Raptor and he earned a reputation as a dedicated and skilled pilot. As Commander of the F-22 Demo Team, Cabo focused on more than just showcasing the aircraft's capabilities. He used his position to inspire others, especially young people, demonstrating the values of resilience, dedication and the pursuit of excellence. Today, Cabo is committed to uplifting the next generation through his work with the Uplift Aviation Foundation, emphasising mentorship and personal growth.

FIVE KEY LESSONS

1. Inspiration Comes from Small Moments

Cabo's love for aviation was sparked by a single airshow as a child, proving how small, impactful moments can shape a person's life.

My Take:

Never underestimate the power of small actions or interactions—they can leave a lasting impression. Whether you're leading a team or inspiring someone new, aim to create those defining moments.

2. Leadership Is About Empowerment

During his time with the F-22 Demo Team, Cabo prioritised hiring the right people, giving them autonomy and offering support when needed.

My Take:

Empowering others fosters trust and collaboration. Great leaders create an environment where their team can excel, knowing they have support when challenges arise.

3. Consistency and Precision Matter

Cabo emphasised the importance of consistency, especially during airshows, where precision in flight maneuvers, narration and timing creates a seamless experience for the audience.

My Take:

In any profession, consistency builds credibility. By refining your skills and striving for precision, you can ensure that your work resonates deeply with your audience or team.

4. Overcoming Challenges Requires Community

Cabo credited his success to the unwavering support of his family and mentors who believed in his vision, even when challenges arose.

My Take:

Surround yourself with people who uplift and believe in you. A strong support network can help you navigate obstacles and achieve your goals.

5. The Power of Mentorship

Through his foundation, Cabo mentors young individuals, using aviation as a tool to inspire and empower them to overcome adversity.

My Take:

Mentorship is a two-way street. By sharing your experiences and guiding others, you grow alongside them. Investing in others' success is one of the most fulfilling things you can do.

APPLYING THE LESSONS TO LIFE

Cabo's journey highlights the transformative power of inspiration, leadership and community. Here are practical ways to apply his lessons:

- **Create meaningful moments:** Look for opportunities to inspire others, whether through small acts of encouragement or sharing your story.

- **Lead with trust:** Hire or collaborate with people you believe in, empower them to excel and offer your guidance when needed.

- **Prioritise precision:** Strive to master your craft and deliver consistently high-quality work.

- **Build your support network:** Surround yourself with people who share your vision and can support you through challenges.

- **Be a mentor:** Share your experiences with those just starting out. Your guidance can make a profound impact on their journey.

APPLY THE LESSONS: REFLECTION QUESTIONS

1. How can you create moments of inspiration for those around you?

2. In what ways can you improve your leadership by empowering others?

3. What areas of your life or work could benefit from greater consistency and precision?

4. Who in your network uplifts and supports you? How can you strengthen those connections?

5. Who could benefit from your mentorship and how can you begin guiding them?

Website, links, projects & contact available on pages 205-214

LOUIS SKUPIEN

CHAPTER 30: JUSTIN "ASTRO" ELLIOTT
TURNING THE THUNDERBIRDS AROUND

INTRODUCTION

Colonel Justin "Astro" Elliott, a distinguished leader in the United States Air Force, shares his inspiring journey through an extraordinary career spanning over two decades. From flying combat missions in the F-15E Strike Eagle to commanding the legendary Thunderbirds demonstration team, Astro exemplifies selflessness, adaptability and a relentless pursuit of excellence. This chapter explores his path, beginning with childhood aspirations of space travel, his rise through the ranks of the Air Force and the difficult decisions that shaped his career. We delve into the lessons of leadership, trust and perseverance that defined his tenure with the Thunderbirds and beyond.

EPISODE SUMMARY

Justin Elliott's story begins in Houston, Texas, where, as a child, he was captivated by the mysteries of space and dreamt of becoming an astronaut. With no military background in his family, Astro's journey was entirely self-driven. After excelling as a Division 1 swimmer and studying mechanical engineering at Yale University, he commissioned into the U.S. Air Force through ROTC, initially believing his poor vision would limit his aspirations to becoming an engineer. A policy change in 2003 allowed laser eye surgery, opening the door for him to pursue his dream of flying.

Astro's career in aviation was stellar, including combat missions in the F-15E Strike Eagle, attending the elite Air Force Weapons School and later transitioning to test piloting advanced aircraft like the F-35. His leadership was solidified when he commanded the 59th Test and Evaluation Squadron, overseeing cutting-edge advancements across multiple fighter jets.

However, his most defining moment came as Thunderbird One, commander and leader of the Thunderbirds demonstration team. Tasked with rebuilding a team struggling culturally and operationally, Astro implemented profound changes to training, hiring and team ethos, transforming the Thunderbirds into a beacon of excellence once again. His story is one of dedication to service, sacrifice and finding fulfilment in uplifting others.

FIVE KEY LESSONS

1. Leadership is Grounded in Trust

The Thunderbirds operate in extreme conditions where trust is non-negotiable. Astro emphasised the importance of "blind trust," fostering a culture where every member could rely completely on one another. This trust was essential for maintaining precision and safety in the air.

My Take: Trust is the bedrock of any successful team. Without it, collaboration falters and performance suffers. Whether leading a family, a business, or a military unit, fostering trust ensures alignment and peak performance.

2. Pursuing Excellence is a Daily Commitment

Astro's mantra for the Thunderbirds was clear: good enough is never enough. Through rigorous training, they pushed themselves beyond perceived limits, focusing on inches rather than miles to achieve extraordinary results.

My Take: True excellence comes from relentless effort and small, incremental improvements. No matter your field, commit daily to refining your craft and you'll find yourself among the elite.

3. The Power of Selflessness

Astro transformed the Thunderbirds 'culture by shifting the focus from individual accomplishments to team and service. The greatest results came when members prioritised the team's mission over personal gain.

My Take: Selflessness inspires trust and fosters unity. By focusing on contributing rather than taking, you create a ripple effect that elevates everyone around you, including yourself.

4. Adapting to Challenges is Essential

Astro took command of the Thunderbirds during a tumultuous time. By identifying root issues, such as cultural drift and outdated training methods, he introduced innovative solutions that redefined how the team operated.

My Take: Challenges are opportunities for growth. Approach them with curiosity and determination and you'll not only overcome them but also emerge stronger and more capable.

5. The Journey is More Rewarding Than the Destination

Despite being a finalist for NASA's astronaut program, Astro chose to step back and lead the Thunderbirds, recognising that the mission and impact mattered more than personal ambition.

My Take: Fulfilment comes not from achieving titles or accolades but from finding purpose in the journey itself. Focus on the intrinsic rewards of your actions and success will follow.

APPLYING THE LESSONS TO LIFE

Justin Elliott's career provides a wealth of actionable insights. Here are some ways to apply his lessons to your own life:

- **Foster trust:** Build environments where people can depend on one another without hesitation.

- **Commit to excellence:** Strive for incremental improvements, even when progress seems slow or unnoticed.

- **Practice selflessness:** Prioritise the mission, the team, or the greater good over personal gain.

- **Adapt to challenges:** See obstacles as opportunities to innovate and grow.

- **Embrace the journey:** Find fulfilment in your purpose, not just your achievements.

APPLY THE LESSONS: REFLECTION QUESTIONS

1. How can you build greater trust within your current team or relationships?

2. In what areas of your life can you commit to incremental improvements?

3. Where can you shift your focus from personal ambition to collective success?

4. What challenges are you currently facing and how can you reframe them as opportunities?

5. Are you finding joy in the process of your work, or are you too focused on the outcome? How can you shift your mindset to embrace the journey?

Website, links, projects & contact available on pages 205-214

CONCLUSION

As we reach the end of 150 Secrets To Greatness, I want to take a moment to reflect on the incredible journey we've taken together. These 30 conversations are more than just interviews; they are deep dives into the minds of some of the most successful, resilient and inspiring people in the world. My hope is that you've found a wealth of wisdom, not only to be inspired by but also to implement into your life. The goal of this book is to create lasting impact by distilling each lesson into clear, actionable takeaways and I believe that if you follow these principles, you'll find greatness in your own life.

The journey doesn't end here—it's only the beginning. Your growth, success and mastery are ongoing processes. Take what you've learned, apply it, adapt it and keep striving toward your goals. The principles in this book have the power to transform your mindset and actions, but they will only work if you do.

The world is full of opportunities, challenges and endless possibilities. As you close this book, remember that greatness is not a destination; it's a continuous pursuit. You've just unlocked a treasure trove of insights from the top performers in various industries, each offering a unique perspective on success. But knowledge without action is meaningless.

The key to making lasting change in your life is to take consistent, deliberate action. Start small, aim high and never stop refining your approach. Whether you're focusing on fitness, business, leadership, or personal growth, the lessons in this book are your blueprint for success. But only you can take the next step.

I encourage you to reflect, adapt and apply these lessons to your life. Greatness doesn't happen overnight, but with persistence and purpose, it is within your reach.

ACTION PLAN TEMPLATE

Here's a simple plan to help you start applying the lessons from 150 Secrets To Greatness in your daily life. Use this as a guideline to break down what you've learned and put it into practice.

Step 1: Choose a Lesson to Focus On

Pick a key takeaway from one of the chapters that resonates with you the most. Whether it's leadership advice, mental toughness, or building resilience, start with one area of focus.

Step 2: Set Clear Goals

Define specific goals related to the lesson you've chosen. For example, if you're focusing on fitness, set a goal to work out 3-4 times a week. If it's about leadership, aim to improve how you communicate with your team or family.

Step 3: Take Daily Action

Create a small, actionable task you can complete each day to move closer to your goal. The key is consistency. Even small actions lead to significant change over time.

Step 4: Track Your Progress

Use a journal, an app, or even just a note on your phone to track your daily progress. It's important to stay accountable and measure how far you've come.

Step 5: Review and Adjust

At the end of each week, reflect on what went well and what could be improved. Adjust your approach as needed to stay on course toward achieving your goals.

CONNECT WITH THE GUESTS

All of my guests have their own ventures, websites, books, services and more that they would love to share with you! Reach out to them, follow their accounts and make sure to support any of the people who helped inspire the best changes or take-home from this book!

1. **Captain Charlie Plumb**

    - **Description:** A former U.S. Navy fighter pilot and Vietnam War POW, Captain Plumb shares powerful lessons in resilience, leadership and mental strength.
    - **Website:** https://www.charlieplumb.com
    - **Instagram:** https://www.instagram.com/plumbtalk

2. **Ramon "CZ" Colón-López**

    - **Description:** Senior Enlisted Advisor to the Chairman of the Joint Chiefs of Staff and a decorated pararescueman with vast special operations experience.
    - **Instagram:** https://www.instagram.com/therealczcolonlopez
    - **Book:** https://www.amazon.com/dp/1lj2jDx

3. **Mark Ormrod**

    - **Description:** Former Royal Marine Commando and triple amputee, Mark Ormrod inspires through his story of positivity, resilience and triumph.
    - **Website:** https://www.markormrod.com
    - **Instagram:** https://www.instagram.com/markormrod
    - **Book:** *Man Down* - https://www.amazon.com/dp/B07QL5FV73

4. **Neil Brown Jr.**

    - **Description:** Actor known for his roles in *SEAL Team* and *Straight Outta Compton,* with a commitment to excellence in the arts.
    - **Instagram:** https://www.instagram.com/neilbrownjr
    - **Watch:** *SEAL Team* on Paramount Plus

5. **Eddie Hamilton**

    - **Description:** A renowned film editor behind blockbuster movies like *Mission: Impossible – Dead Reckoning.*
    - **Website:** https://eddiehamilton.com
    - **Watch:** *Mission: Impossible – Dead Reckoning*

6. **Michelle "Mace" Curran**

   - **Description:** Former lead solo pilot for the Thunderbirds, now an inspirational speaker and advocate for overcoming adversity.
   - **Website:** https://macecurran.com
   - **Instagram:** https://www.instagram.com/mace_curran

7. **Kegan "Smurf" Gill**

   - **Description:** Retired U.S. Air Force pararescueman and author of *Phoenix Revival*, focused on recovery and resilience.
   - **Instagram:** https://www.instagram.com/kegansmurfgill
   - **Book:** *Phoenix Revival*

8. **Rich Graham**

   - **Description:** Former Navy SEAL and founder of Full Spectrum Warrior, offering tactical training and fitness programs.
   - **Website:** https://fullspectrumwarriors.com
   - **Instagram:** https://www.instagram.com/fullspectrumwarriorusa
   - **YouTube:** https://www.youtube.com/c/RichGraham

9. Mark Divine

- **Description:** Retired Navy SEAL Commander, mental toughness expert and bestselling author.
- **Website:** https://markdivine.com
- **Instagram:** https://www.instagram.com/realmarkdivine

10. Taylor "Fema" Hiester

- **Description:** Pilot for the U.S. Air Force F-16 Viper Demonstration Team, showcasing precision and teamwork in aviation.
- **Instagram:** https://www.instagram.com/femahiester
- **Team Instagram:** https://www.instagram.com/f16viperdemoteam

11. Tucker "Cinco" Hamilton

- **Description:** U.S. Air Force test pilot and commander, advancing aerospace innovation and AI in aviation.
- **Instagram:** https://www.instagram.com/cincohamilton

12. Tyler Grey

- **Description:** Former Army Ranger turned actor, known for his portrayal of authenticity in *SEAL Team*.
- **Instagram:** https://www.instagram.com/tyleragrey

- **Watch:** *SEAL Team*

13. Eric Lee

- **Description:** Talented musician with heartfelt compositions, including the hit "Always On My Mind."
- **Website:** https://ericlee.music
- **Instagram:** https://www.instagram.com/ericleemusic
- **Listen to:** *Always On My Mind*

14. Anthony Smith

- **Description:** Creative producer, known for crafting engaging trailers for *Diary Of A CEO*.
- **Instagram:** https://www.instagram.com/anthonyr.smith

15. Kirk Lippold

- **Description:** Former Commander of the USS Cole, author and speaker on leadership and resilience.
- **LinkedIn:** https://www.linkedin.com/in/kirk-lippold-5421967
- **Facebook:** https://www.facebook.com/kirk.lippold.9
- **Book:** *Front Burner: Al Qaeda's Attack on the USS Cole* - https://www.amazon.com/dp/B007FRXDYI

16. Tim Parlatore

- **Description:** Attorney and founder of Parlatore Law Group, specialising in legal innovation and strategy.
- **Website:** https://parlatorelawgroup.com
- **Instagram:** https://www.instagram.com/tparlatore

17. Samuel "RaZZ" Larson

- **Description:** Pilot and commander of the F-22 Raptor Demo Team, showcasing cutting-edge air power.
- **Instagram:** https://www.instagram.com/razzlarson
- **Team Instagram:** https://www.instagram.com/f22demoteam

18. Greg "Boss" Wooldridge

- **Description:** Former Commander of the Blue Angels, Greg Wooldridge leads with precision and trust.
- **Website:** https://johnfoleyinc.com/greg-boss-wooldridge
- **LinkedIn:** https://www.linkedin.com/in/greg-boss-wooldridge

19. Kris "Tanto" Paronto

- **Description:** Former CIA contractor and co-author of *13 Hours*, recounting the Benghazi attack.

- **Website:** https://kristantoparonto.com
- **Instagram:** https://www.instagram.com/real_kris_tanto_paronto

20. Trey Rawls

- **Description:** Experienced leader and consultant, focused on advancing organisational excellence.
- **LinkedIn:** https://www.linkedin.com/in/trey-rawls-4a07199

21. Eddie Penney

- **Description:** Former Navy SEAL and author of *Unafraid: Staring Down Terror as a Navy SEAL and Single Dad*, sharing his journey of resilience.
- **Website:** https://eddiepenney.com
- **Book:** https://www.amazon.com/dp/19V1XWD

22. Lance Power

- **Description:** Command Chief of the 67th Cyberspace Wing, United States Air Force, specialising in cybersecurity and leadership.
- **LinkedIn:** https://www.linkedin.com/in/lance-power

23. Matthew "Whiz" Buckley

- **Description:** Former Top Gun pilot, motivational speaker and founder of the No Fallen Heroes Foundation.
- **Website:** https://whizbuckley.com
- **Foundation:** https://nofallenheroesfoundation.org
- **Programs:** https://topgunoptions.com
- **Instagram:** https://www.instagram.com/officialwhizbuckley

24. Helen Isaac

- **Description:** Fitness entrepreneur and founder of Helfit, inspiring others through health and wellness.
- **Website:** https://helfit.co.uk
- **Instagram:** https://www.instagram.com/helenifitness

25. Jon "Fizzle" Fay

- **Description:** Executive Officer of the U.S. Navy's Blue Angels, leading with precision and trust.
- **LinkedIn:** https://www.linkedin.com/in/jon-fay
- **Instagram:** https://www.instagram.com/centerpoint_solutions_llc

26. Craig Harrison

- **Description:** Former British Army sniper and world record holder for the longest confirmed sniper kill.
- **Website:** https://www.themavericksurvivalschool.co.uk
- **Instagram:** https://www.instagram.com/cohcraigharrison

27. Miles Daisher

- **Description:** Renowned BASE jumper and skydiver, known for pushing the limits of human flight.
- **Website:** https://www.milesdaisher.com
- **Instagram:** https://www.instagram.com/miles_daisher

28. Michael Sarraille

- **Description:** Retired Navy SEAL, author and speaker on leadership and performance optimisation.
- **Website:** https://mikesarraille.com
- **Instagram:** https://www.instagram.com/mr.sarraille

29. Joshua "Cabo" Gunderson

- **Description:** F-22 Raptor Demo Team pilot and commander, representing cutting-edge aviation excellence.
- **Instagram:** https://www.instagram.com/cabogunderson

- **LinkedIn:** https://www.linkedin.com/in/joshuacabogunderson

- **Bio:** https://www.jble.af.mil/About-Us/Biographies/Display/Article/2065359/maj-joshua-cabo-gunderson

- **Demo Team Info:** https://www.airforceheritageflight.org/news/maj-josh-cabo-gunderson-named-new-f-22-raptor-demo-team-pilot

- **YouTube:** https://www.youtube.com/@CaboGunderson22

30. Justin "Astro" Elliott

- **Description:** Aerospace leader and innovator with extensive operational and leadership experience.

- **LinkedIn:** https://www.linkedin.com/in/justin-elliott-7a35307b

REFLECTION QUESTIONS FOR THE WHOLE BOOK

Use these reflection questions to deepen your understanding of the lessons and how you can apply them in your life:

- Which key takeaway or lesson from the book had the biggest impact on you? Why?

- What is one area of your life where you can immediately apply the principles shared by the guests?

- How will you incorporate these lessons into your daily habits or routines?

- Have you faced challenges similar to those discussed by the guests? How did you handle them?

- What steps will you take to measure your progress and growth as you begin to apply these lessons?

- What is one goal you can set today that aligns with the advice in this book?

- How will you hold yourself accountable for making consistent progress?

- Which guest's story resonated with you the most and how can their journey inspire your own?

LOUIS SKUPIEN

THIS ONE IS FOR YOU!

To each of you who has picked up this book—thank you. Your decision to read *150 Secrets To Greatness* shows a commitment to bettering yourself and striving for excellence in your life. I hope the lessons you've learned here serve as a catalyst for growth and success in whatever path you choose.

You are the reason I've put this work together. Your belief in the power of learning from the best, distilling those lessons and applying them is what drives me to continue sharing these incredible conversations. Thank you for being a part of this journey with me. Let's keep pushing the boundaries of what's possible and never stop reaching for greatness.

This is just the beginning. The conversations in this book are a part of an ongoing series of interviews from the *TALK4* Podcast and as I continue to connect with high performers across the globe, there will be more to come.

In the next volume of *150 Secrets To Greatness*, I'll share insights from even more top performers across a diverse range of industries, bringing you their best advice, distilled into actionable steps. So, stay tuned for the next instalment, where we'll delve deeper into the minds of those at the pinnacle of success.

In the meantime, I'll continue to bring you fresh conversations on the *TALK4* Podcast. Make sure to subscribe and follow on your favourite platform so you never miss an episode—and who knows, maybe you'll see some familiar faces featured in the next book!

LOUIS SKUPIEN

GLOSSARY OF KEY TERMS, ORGANISATIONS AND CONCEPTS

Throughout *150 Secrets To Greatness*, you'll encounter various terms, organisations and concepts related to leadership, performance and personal development. This glossary is designed to provide clarity and deepen your understanding of these key ideas.

KEY CONCEPTS

Actionable Takeaways

Clear, specific steps or lessons that can be immediately applied to your life to achieve tangible results.

Adaptability

The ability to adjust and respond to changing conditions, challenges, or environments. A key trait of high performers and resilient individuals.

Accountability

Holding oneself or others responsible for actions, decisions, or outcomes. A crucial element in leadership, teamwork and personal growth.

Adversity

Difficulties or misfortunes that challenge an individual's strength, resilience and mindset. Overcoming adversity is a recurring theme in high-performance environments.

AI (Artificial Intelligence)

A field of computer science that aims to create systems capable of performing tasks that typically require human intelligence, such as learning, decision-making and problem-solving. Discussed in the context of cutting-edge military and business applications.

Continuous Improvement

The ongoing effort to enhance skills, processes, or outcomes. High performers commit to continuous improvement to stay at the top of their game.

Decision-Making Under Pressure

The ability to make clear, rational decisions in high-stress or high-stakes situations. This is a crucial skill in both military operations and business leadership.

Discipline

The practice of training oneself to follow a specific code of behaviour or work ethic, often involving consistent effort, self-control and focus.

Emotional Resilience

The capacity to recover from stress, adversity, or trauma while maintaining a positive outlook. This trait is key for success in personal and professional life.

Failure as Growth

The concept that failure is not the end, but a valuable learning experience that helps refine skills and strategies for future success.

Leadership

The ability to guide, inspire and influence others toward a common goal. Effective leadership is a recurring theme throughout the book, discussed by top performers in military, business and creative fields.

Mental Toughness

The ability to stay focused, composed and effective under pressure. Mental toughness is essential for high performance in both sports and professional settings.

Mindset

A mental framework or belief system that influences how an individual approaches challenges and opportunities. High performers cultivate a growth mindset, focusing on learning and development.

Nutrition Science

The study of how diet and nutrients affect health, performance and well-being. In this book, experts discuss how to cut through myths and apply evidence-based strategies for optimal nutrition.

Resilience

The capacity to recover quickly from difficulties and adapt to challenging circumstances. A core concept discussed by several guests, particularly those with military backgrounds.

Self-Reflection

The process of examining one's own thoughts, feelings and actions in order to gain insight and improve. Many guests highlight the importance of self-reflection in achieving personal and professional growth.

Special Operations

Elite military units trained to conduct missions that are beyond the scope of conventional forces. Several guests in the book come from Special Operations backgrounds, sharing insights into leadership, discipline and mental toughness.

Strategic Thinking

The ability to plan and execute long-term goals by anticipating challenges and adapting to evolving circumstances. Often discussed in the context of leadership and decision-making.

Team Building

The process of developing a cohesive, high-performing group. Team building requires strong communication, shared values and trust, all of which are highlighted in various chapters.

Visualisation

A mental technique used by athletes, military personnel and business leaders to improve performance by imagining success and rehearsing actions in the mind before executing them in reality.

KEY TEAMS, ORGANISATIONS, PODCAST TERMS & FIGHTER PILOT PHRASES.

Blue Angels

The U.S. Navy's elite flight demonstration squadron known for their precise aerobatic manoeuvres and teamwork. A symbol of naval aviation excellence, discussed by guests such as Jon 'Fizzle' Fay.

Thunderbirds

The U.S. Air Force's aerial demonstration team, showcasing the capabilities of modern military jets while inspiring audiences around the world. Featured in episodes with pilots like Michelle "Mace" Curran.

Patriots Jet Team

A civilian aerobatic display team that performs complex manoeuvres at airshows, often flying in L-39 jets. Known for their precision, they play a key role in some of the podcast's aviation-related content.

U.S. Navy SEALs

The U.S. Navy's Special Operations force, specialising in unconventional warfare, counter-terrorism and direct action missions. Guests such as Mark Divine and Eddie Penney share insights from their experiences in this elite group.

SEALFIT

A physical and mental training program founded by Mark Divine, designed to help people develop strength, mental toughness and resilience. SEALFIT's approach combines the warrior mindset with holistic training.

Unbeatable Mind

A program also founded by Mark Divine that focuses on developing mental toughness, emotional resilience and leadership skills through practices like meditation and visualisation.

USAF Pararescue (PJ)

Elite combat search and rescue specialists, known for saving lives in combat and humanitarian missions. Guests like Ramon "CZ" Colon

Lopez come from this highly respected branch of U.S. Special Operations.

F-22 Raptor Demo Team

The U.S. Air Force team that demonstrates the capabilities of the F-22 Raptor, one of the most advanced fighter jets in the world. Featured in conversations with Samuel "RaZZ" Larson, who leads this team.

Rhino Demo Team

A U.S. Navy squadron showcasing the abilities of the F/A-18 Super Hornet. The Rhino Demo Team provides insights into advanced military aviation and is a key topic of discussion in episodes with pilots like Evan "Squints" Goss.

U.S. Marine Corps

A branch of the U.S. Armed Forces that specialises in expeditionary and amphibious warfare. Several guests, including Nick "Machine" Lavery, share their experiences as Marines and lessons in leadership and resilience.

British Army

The principal land warfare force of the United Kingdom. Guests such as Craig Harrison, a sniper world-record holder, share lessons from their service in the British Army.

Joint Chiefs of Staff (JCS)

The senior leadership body that advises the President of the United States and the Secretary of Defence on military matters. Ramon "CZ" Colon Lopez served as Senior Enlisted Advisor to the Chairman, providing unique leadership insights.

Afterburner: A component on some jet engines that provides an extra burst of power by injecting fuel directly into the exhaust stream, creating additional thrust

Dogfight: A close-range, high-speed aerial battle between fighter aircraft

Formation Flying: A coordinated flight pattern where multiple aircraft fly together in a specific arrangement, often seen in military displays and training missions.

G-Force: The force of acceleration felt by a pilot when manoeuvring an aircraft, measured in multiples of Earth's gravity (e.g., 2G, 9G).

Wingman: A pilot who supports the lead pilot in a formation. Being a good wingman requires strong communication and situational awareness.

Sortie: A single mission or flight by a military aircraft, usually as part of a larger operation.

Call Sign: A nickname or code name given to a fighter pilot. Many of Louis 'podcast guests from the aviation world have unique call signs, such as "RaZZ" Larson or "Cinco" Hamilton.

TALK4 Podcast: Louis Skupien's podcast, where he interviews top performers from various industries, asking four key questions to extract valuable insights and lessons.

Episode: A single recording in a podcast series. Each episode of TALK4 focuses on a different high-performing individual.

Transcription: The written version of the spoken audio from a podcast episode. Transcriptions are often used for accessibility and repurposing content.

Host: The individual who presents the podcast and engages in conversations with guests. Louis Skupien is the host of TALK4.

Subscriber: A person who follows a podcast to receive automatic updates when new episodes are released.

Monetisation: The process of earning revenue from a podcast, usually through sponsorships, advertisements, or listener support

GET FIT ANYWHERE IN THE WORLD WITH FORTIS FIT!

Looking to achieve your fitness goals from anywhere in the world? Fortis Fit offers an innovative, app-based online personal training experience tailored to your needs—no matter where you are.

At Fortis Fit, we provide custom workout plans, nutritional guidance and ongoing support to help you reach your fitness goals. Whether you're looking to build strength, lose weight, or enhance your overall health, our app-based approach means you can train at your own pace, anytime, anywhere.

WHY CHOOSE FORTIS FIT?

- **Personalised Training Plans:** Each program is tailored to your unique fitness level, preferences and goals.

- **Expert Guidance:** Train with certified personal trainers, including the founder, Louis Skupien, who is passionate about helping you succeed.

- **Flexible Workouts:** No gym? No problem! We provide at-home and gym-based plans that work around your lifestyle.

- **Accessible to Everyone:** Whether you're a beginner or an advanced athlete, Fortis Fit is designed to help you achieve results, wherever you are.

- **24/7 Support:** Stay connected with your trainer and get the motivation and tips you need through the app.

START YOUR FITNESS JOURNEY TODAY!

Head over to **FortisFitUK.com** and sign up for the most flexible, comprehensive and results-driven online training program available.

Your goals, your schedule—transformed with Fortis Fit.

WELCOME TO ANVIL TACTICAL AIRSOFT - YOUR ULTIMATE AIRSOFT GEAR DESTINATION!

At Anvil Tactical Airsoft, we are dedicated to providing you with the highest quality Airsoft gear and equipment. Whether you're a beginner or a seasoned pro, we've got everything you need to elevate your game and dominate the field.

WHY CHOOSE ANVIL TACTICAL AIRSOFT?

- **Premium Gear:** We offer a wide range of Airsoft guns, tactical gear and accessories from trusted brands.

- **Expert Advice:** Our team of Airsoft enthusiasts is here to help you choose the right gear for your style of play.

- **Durability & Performance:** Our products are built to last and designed to enhance your performance in the field.

- **Wide Selection:** From rifles and pistols to tactical vests and face protection, we've got you covered.

SPECIAL OFFER: GET 10% OFF!

As a thank you for being part of the Anvil Tactical Airsoft community, we're offering **10% off your purchase** with the code **ANVIL10** at checkout. Whether you're gearing up for your next battle or upgrading your current load-out, now is the perfect time to grab the best gear at an unbeatable price!

Visit **AnvilTacticalAirsoft.com** to explore our collection and take your Airsoft game to the next level. Don't forget to use code **ANVIL10** for your 10% discount.

Printed in Great Britain
by Amazon